# GREAT TRADITIONAL STYLE

MEREDITH® BOOKS
DES MOINES, IOWA

*Great Traditional Style*
Contributing Writer: Shelley Stewart
Contributing Researcher: Wanda Ventling
Contributing Graphic Designer: Sundie Ruppert, Studio G
Assistant Art Director: Erin Burns
Copy Chief: Terri Fredrickson
Publishing Operations Manager: Karen Schirm
Senior Editor, Asset & Information Management: Phillip Morgan
Edit and Design Production Coordinator: Mary Lee Gavin
Editorial Assistant: Kaye Chabot
Book Production Managers: Pam Kvitne, Marjorie J. Schenkelberg,
 Rick von Holdt, Mark Weaver
Contributing Copy Editor: Jane Woychick
Contributing Proofreaders: Sara Henderson, Ellen Modersohn,
 Mary Helen Schiltz
Contributing Cover Photographer: Ed Gohlich
Contributing Indexer: Sharon Duffy

**Meredith® Books**
Executive Director, Editorial: Gregory H. Kayko
Executive Director, Design: Matt Strelecki
Managing Editor: Amy Tincher-Durik
Senior Editor/Group Manager: Vicki Leigh Ingham
Senior Associate Design Director: Mick Schnepf
Marketing Product Manager: Steve Rogers

Publisher and Editor in Chief: James D. Blume
Editorial Director: Linda Raglan Cunningham
Executive Director, Marketing: Steve Malone
Executive Director, New Business Development: Todd M. Davis
Executive Director, Sales: Ken Zagor
Director, Operations: George A. Susral
Director, Production: Douglas M. Johnston
Director, Marketing: Amy Nichols
Business Director: Jim Leonard

Vice President and General Manager: Douglas J. Guendel

**Meredith Publishing Group**
President: Jack Griffin
Executive Vice President: Bob Mate

**Meredith Corporation**
Chairman and Chief Executive Officer: William T. Kerr
President and Chief Operating Officer: Stephen M. Lacy

In Memoriam: E.T. Meredith III (1933–2003)

All of us at Meredith® Books are dedicated to providing you with information and ideas to enhance your home. We welcome your comments and suggestions. Write to us at: Meredith Books, Home Decorating and Design Editorial Department, 1716 Locust St., Des Moines, IA 50309-3023.

# TABLE OF CONTENTS

Close your eyes and imagine the quintessential traditional home. What comes to mind? Grand Irish manors, English country gardens, and the dazzling homes of landed gentry where crystal chandeliers, elaborate moldings, and curving staircases are the rule? In much of the Western world, traditional style refers to the formal elegance preferred by well-to-do 18th-century families in Great Britain, with a few French, Italian, German, Dutch, or Swedish touches as well.

It's important to remember that even in the 18th century, no one style fit all. There were city homes and country homes, palatial estates and modest cottages. When the style jumped the Atlantic and came to newly colonized America, more differences appeared. Even now, the style is evolving—it's more relaxed, less formal, more individual—so it's back to the question: What is traditional style? This book explores its many interpretations.

You've undoubtedly heard these terms: Queen Anne, Georgian, Regency, rococo, neoclassical, Chippendale, Hepplewhite. Familiar names, but what do they signify?

Because so much of traditional design came from England, a quick look at her history is helpful. There were four kings named George, beginning with George I, a slow-witted relative of Queen Elizabeth I who was brought from Germany in 1714 to be king of England, even though he spoke no English.

His son, King George II, who reigned from 1727–1760, fancied the trappings of being king but left the running of the country to politicians, which was probably a good thing. He devoted himself to a dizzy social whirl between country estates. In the meantime, prosperous England was establishing trade all over the world.

His son, George III, reigned from 1760–1820, presiding over the loss of the American Colonies. He suffered from bouts of mental illness so severe that finally Parliament installed his son to rule as Prince Regent. Also named George, the Regent was an extravagant, pleasure-seeking fop who built frivolous structures such as the Brighton Pavilion while England was in the throes of both the Napoleonic Wars and the early Industrial Revolution.

Today, the term *Georgian* refers to the period between 1717 and 1830 when the "Georges" were in power. Queen Anne, who ruled only briefly before George I, bestowed her name on a graceful style that, along with early- and mid-Georgian styles, became known as rococo, influencing art and music as well as architecture and the decorative arts. Late Georgian belongs to the neoclassical period in art and architecture, characterized by a return to classical motifs inspired by archeological finds in Italy.

Relating traditional furnishings to the personalities of the four Georges is an easy way to remember their characteristics. Very early 18th-century furniture was heavy and dark, with Northern European influences. When George II came along, England was stable, and large country houses built to impress others needed huge quantities of fine furnishings. Design and artistry, influenced by exotic India and China, flourished in the hands of skilled craftsmen.

This continued under George III, but the purity of traditional style was slightly diluted by its move to America. Then, under the Regency, it became more whimsical, gaining details that now seem charmingly lighthearted.

Two furniture makers stand out: Thomas Chippendale and George Hepplewhite. In 1754 Chippendale published an influential book of designs with fanciful Chinese, Gothic, and French rococo elements that included latticework, carvings, and interlaced forms. Hepplewhite, his slightly later contemporary, favored painted and inlaid decoration, tapering reeded or fluted legs, and the spade foot. Shield, lyre, or oval backs, Prince-of-Wales feathers, ribbons, and rosettes gave his pieces a distinctive look.

That's the background of great traditional style—with the home as a setting for ladies and gentlemen with fine sensibilities and well-bred behavior. After almost 300 years, this style, with its broad variations, is still extremely popular. Rooted in history and heritage, the look successfully marries elegance with comfort. Browse through the following pages for inspiring ideas that can bring that comfortable elegance to your home.

**COLOR CHOICES** IN GEORGIAN TIMES, COLOR IN PAINT CAME FROM NATURAL SOURCES—BARK AND OTHER PLANT MATERIALS, MINERALS, AND SHELLS WERE GROUND UP AND THEIR PIGMENTS MIXED WITH OIL AND SOMETIMES MILK. OCHER YELLOW, WALNUT BROWN, INDIGO BLUE, AND MADDER RED, PLUS ALL OF THEIR COMBINATIONS, WERE POPULAR COLORS. WHITE LEAD MIXED WITH THESE COULD PRODUCE PASTEL TINTS.

FABRICS, TOO, COULD ONLY BE MADE IN SUCH COLORS UNTIL THE ADVENT OF ANILINE DYES IN 1856, WHICH INTRODUCED GARISH COLORS AND COMBINATIONS THAT WOULD SHOCK MODERN SENSIBILITIES. TODAY'S TRADITIONAL HOMES USE EVERY COLOR, OFTEN A STEP OR TWO AWAY FROM STRICTLY AUTHENTIC, BUT ALWAYS IN STEP WITH THE SPIRIT OF THE STYLE. COLORS RANGE FROM PASTEL OR NEUTRALS TO COBALT BLUE, RASPBERRY RED, AND YELLOW. UNLESS THE HOME IS A HISTORIC RESTORATION, COLOR IS A PERSONAL CHOICE.

**FLOORS AND WALLS** THE MOST AUTHENTIC HOMES USE ONLY MATERIALS AVAILABLE IN THE 18TH CENTURY. FOR FLOORS, THESE INCLUDE BRICK, LIMESTONE, AND MARBLE—WITH OR WITHOUT CONTRASTING ACCENT PIECES. OR TRY WOOD FLOORING IN OAK, CHERRY, OR WALNUT, LAID PARALLEL OR IN A HERRINGBONE PATTERN.

MOLDING, OFTEN IN CRISP WHITE OR OFF-WHITE, IS KEY TO CREATING TRADITIONAL-STYLE WALLS. FORMAL ROOMS HAVE RAISED PANELING, WAINSCOTING, AND DENTIL OR CARVED MOLDINGS. EVEN INFORMAL ROOMS HAVE DEEP BASE MOLDING AND CROWN MOLDING. NATURAL-WOOD PANELING IS ALWAYS APPROPRIATE, ESPECIALLY IN MASCULINE STUDIES OR LIBRARIES.

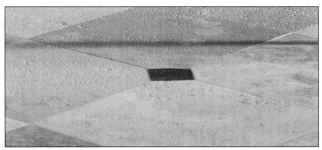

FABRICS In the Georgian period, Europe moved from solid-color wool and linen fabrics with applied trimmings to fabrics with texture and pattern. Trade with Asia introduced Oriental rugs, soft cashmere, and cotton batiks with wax-resist designs. The East India Company brought back imports of Chinese brocade and silk. By 1716, numerous laws prohibited importing printed cottons and silks to England—intending to protect the domestic fabric industry—but the public clamored for them anyway.

The French took the lead in producing these fabrics in Europe, first printing calico in 1794. When Napoleon captured a cannon in battle, an enterprising businessman turned it into a fabric roller, thus helping to create the toile de Jouy fabric industry. With the Industrial Revolution, innovation came fast. Soon velvet, damask, silk, satin, taffeta, calico, and chintz were priced for the popular market. Only durability determines which of these fabrics is appropriate for draperies or upholstery.

PATTERNS The Georgian period saw an explosion in pattern as technological advances made a variety of weaves and printing techniques possible. Solids and stripes gave way to woven patterns and soon fabric could even be printed to mimic other materials.

Heavy Jacobean designs with stylized vines and flowers evolved to more delicate, trailing floral patterns. Toile de Jouy, in fabric or wallpaper, sprang up with large-scale pastoral scenes, often in red, blue, or green on an off-white ground. Documentary wallpapers reflect specific historical periods. Chinese-inspired designs and bamboo motifs were very popular, as were teardrop-shape paisley motifs, especially in England. In France, the bumblebee—symbol of Napoleon—and fleur-de-lis motifs were popular.

FURNITURE Furniture can be as formal or informal as you like, but traditional features include curving cabriole legs, carved back splats, ball-and-claw feet on chairs, and broken-arch or scrolled pediment tops on chests of drawers. Walnut, cherry, and mahogany were the woods of choice historically, always polished and sometimes with satin-wood inlay, painting, or gilding. The same styles in light oak or pine create a more casual look.

Early Georgian-style furniture is characterized by carved and pierced surfaces. Late Georgian style, which corresponds to the American Federal or neoclassical period, features smooth, highly polished surfaces embellished with inlay, clean lines, simple silhouettes, and slender legs. Upholstered wing chairs, originally designed to allow the sick to sleep upright, have become a staple of traditional living rooms. Whether you buy antiques or reproductions, look for elegance, symmetry, and attention to detail.

RUGS AND ACCESSORIES Wall-to-wall carpeting is a definite "no." Go with rugs instead. Oriental rugs are a popular choice, and they needn't be in like-new condition; if the pile is worn or the dyes are bleached by the sun, it could be because the rugs are family heirlooms (always desirable). Pastel Aubusson, Savonnerie, and needlepoint rugs are other good choices. Sisal rugs, while not authentic, have a pleasing simplicity in casual rooms.

For lighting, use crystal or multibranched chandeliers in antique styles. Combine china with pewter or silver serving pieces, depending on formality, and add crystal stemware and silverware for table settings. Blue and white Delft or Chinese-export porcelain, Staffordshire pottery, bronzes, marble statues, and similar accessories add a luxurious note. Choose natural wood or gilded frames. Never devalue an antique mirror by resilvering it; just enjoy its mottled beauty.

# 1
## Stately Revival

# Relaxed Elegance

## A stately Georgian-style home bends its rules for an active family with young children.

OPPOSITE An antique French Aubusson rug inspired the soft, muted colors in the living room. The focal point is a 19th-century American painting, whose vivid blues appear in other accessories as well.

LEFT In the dining room, an elaborate crystal chandelier is as decorative in the daytime as it is at night. Fresh flowers accent the peach-tone walls.

OPPOSITE ORNATE TREAD BRACKETS AND TURNED SPINDLES EMPHASIZE THE DRAMATIC SWEEP OF THE STAIRCASE IN THE ENTRY.

LEFT THE 1930S GEORGIAN-STYLE HOME REVEALS ITS ENGLISH ARCHITECTURAL ROOTS IN THE SYMMETRICAL FACADE WITH A PROJECTING CENTER SECTION CAPPED BY A TRIANGULAR PEDIMENT. BROAD STEPS LEADING TO A PORTICOED DOOR AND A PAIR OF CHIMNEYS FLANKING THE HIPPED ROOF ARE ALSO INDICATIVE OF THE STYLE.

Festooned with ivy, this 1930s brick home on the eastern shore of Maryland is surrounded by 106 acres of verdant landscape with spectacular views of the Chesapeake Bay. Used as a hunting lodge by former owners, it hosted countless gatherings of cigar-smoking movers and shakers in its 10,000 square feet of formally appointed rooms. Since 1997, though, the venerable old house has changed. With new owners and the help of Baltimore interior designer Mona Hajj, it has become the vacation home for a family that includes two children. Sleepovers with their friends have replaced gentlemen's hunting weekends, and although the demeanor of the house remains elegant, its interiors are far more family friendly.

Before beginning the transformation, Hajj engaged the homeowners in long discussions about how they wanted to live in the house. They asked for traditional interiors that allowed for comfort, and she responded with a mixture of European antiques and newer upholstered pieces combined with carefully chosen artwork. (CONTINUED ON PAGE 19)

ABOVE THE GLEAMING GEORGE III SIDEBOARD ANCHORS AN ENGLISH OIL PAINTING. THE PAINTING, A ROMANTICIZED LANDSCAPE, IS TYPICAL OF ARTWORK FROM THE LATE 18TH CENTURY.

RIGHT THE ROUND TABLE SEATS AS MANY AS 16 GUESTS, SO ALL CAN PARTICIPATE IN LIVELY CONVERSATION. TWO COZY CHAIRS IN FRONT OF THE FIREPLACE ENCOURAGE MORE-INTIMATE TALKS.

OPPOSITE THE DOUBLE-BONNET SECRETARY, MADE FROM ENGLISH WALNUT, IS A 19TH-CENTURY PIECE THAT WAS FOUND IN NEW YORK. NOW IN THE FOYER, IT PROVIDES DISPLAY SPACE FOR A COLORFUL RUSSIAN TEACUP COLLECTION AND A 19TH-CENTURY NAUTICAL PAINTING BY ALBERT BIERSTADT.

RIGHT INLAID WOOD, LOCKABLE DRAWERS, AND SIMPLE BRONZE PULLS ARE CLASSIC ADORNMENTS ON EARLY 19TH-CENTURY FURNITURE. THE SYMMETRICAL ARRANGEMENT OF PAINTINGS, PORCELAIN, AND CANDLESTICKS ON THE BOMBÉ CHEST IS ALSO TYPICAL OF THE REGENCY AESTHETIC.

"My main goal was to incorporate comfortable elegance with the beautiful natural light and broad water views," Hajj says. The Georgian-style exterior and the characteristically ornate woodwork inside the home require a certain formality in the interiors, yet whenever possible, Hajj chose furnishings that were nonintimidating and durable enough to withstand active use.

Often using one of the family's sun-washed antique rugs as inspiration, Hajj chose mainly warm colors and painted several rooms in luscious shades of salmon and creamy yellow. "The rug is really the heart and soul of the room, and that's usually where I start," Hajj says. "Then I go around to the walls, to the ceiling, and back to the floor." The woodwork and moldings are primarily a creamy shade of white for design continuity.

LEFT THE SUNNY
CONSERVATORY, NOW
USED AS A FAMILY ROOM,
HAS WICKER AND WOOD
FURNITURE WITH
DURABLE COTTON
CUSHIONS THAT ARE
ALMOST IMPERVIOUS TO
HEAVY USE AND
CHILDREN'S ACTIVITIES.

Fabrics are classic—crisp stripes and rich brocades in the more formal living and dining rooms and plaids or muted prints in private areas and rooms the children are likely to frequent. In the casual family room, slipcovered cushions have a tailored appearance yet the covers easily slip off for cleaning when necessary. "The homeowners wanted a room where their children would be able to jump on the furniture or spill milk, and nobody would care because it wouldn't hurt a thing," Hajj says.

The family feels that even though some of the pieces may be quite valuable, the children shouldn't be restricted in their own home, so they are allowed in every room. Indeed, by growing up surrounded by quality, they're learning to live with fine furnishings and to treat them with respect. They've also discovered that the space beneath the antique dining table makes a wonderful hiding place during an indoor game of hide-and-seek.

OPPOSITE WHEN HE ENLARGED THE ORIGINAL 1930S KITCHEN, ARCHITECT WAYNE GOOD CREATED SPACE FOR A HUGE ENGLISH-PINE ISLAND THAT DOUBLES AS A BREAKFAST BAR. COPPER POTS ARE WITHIN EASY REACH ON THE CUSTOM-MADE IRON POT RACK OVERHEAD.

LEFT SITUATED ON 106 ACRES ON THE EASTERN SHORE OF MARYLAND, THE HOUSE ENJOYS WONDERFUL VIEWS OF CHESAPEAKE BAY. THIS NEWLY BUILT OUTDOOR ROOM ACTS AS AN EXTENSION OF THE HOUSE AND HAS QUICKLY TURNED INTO A FAVORITE GATHERING SPOT.

The dining table is viewed as the heart of the home because its ample circumference seats up to 16 family members or other guests for entertaining. Despite its size, the table creates an intimate feeling in the room: Its shape encourages interaction, and everyone is within easy view. Above the huge table, an equally impressive antique chandelier is decked out in hundreds of sparkling crystal prisms that amplify the light.

Another favored spot for entertaining is the new alfresco room that architect Wayne Good added, using high walls with exceptional brickwork and details to meld it seamlessly with the original architecture of the home. Furnished with durable Chippendale-style teak furniture, the outdoor room blends beautifully with styles inside the house. The spacious area is perfect for impromptu warm-weather meals, games of hopscotch, or outdoor activities on a rainy day. The addition is another instance of relaxation taking precedence over formality in this family-friendly vacation home.

ABOVE AN ANTIQUE
FRENCH CHEST HAS
BEEN CONVERTED TO A
VANITY IN ONE OF THE
TWO MASTER BATHS. THE
REPRODUCTION BATHTUB
IS A CLASSIC EARLY-20TH-
CENTURY STYLE.

RIGHT CARVED OUT OF
FORMERLY UNUSED ATTIC
SPACE, THIS GUEST ROOM
FEATURES AN ANTIQUE
FRENCH BED AND WARM
CORAL WALLS.

# Historic Connection

A YOUNG RICHMOND COUPLE WITH TWO SMALL CHILDREN PUTS DOWN ROOTS IN A HOME KNOWN FOR ITS FINE ARCHITECTURE AND ITS ROLE IN COMMUNITY AFFAIRS.

LEFT THE INITIALS OF THE NEW BABY ARE HAND-PAINTED ON THE FIREPLACE MANTEL IN HER ROOM.

OPPOSITE ANTIQUE SILVER GOBLETS SOMETIMES SERVE AS INDIVIDUAL VASES FOR THE PARTIES AND CIVIC FUND-RAISERS THE FRENCHES HOST IN THEIR ELEGANT GEORGIAN REVIVAL HOME.

LEFT THE MUTED PALETTE OF CAFÉ AU LAIT, SOFT AQUA, AND ROSE COMES FROM EMBROIDERED DRAPERY FABRIC AT THE LIVING ROOM WINDOWS.

RIGHT THE FRENCHES' 1918 GEORGIAN-REVIVAL HOME, WESTBOURNE, IS CONSIDERED BY MANY TO BE THE FINEST EXAMPLE OF ITS STYLE IN VIRGINIA.

PAGES 30–31 BROAD STRIPES CREATE A STATELY BACKDROP FOR CONTEMPORARY ART IN THE ENTRY. THE PAIR OF REGENCY-STYLE SETTEES CAME FROM LOCAL FURNITURE DESIGNER HARRISON HIGGINS.

If a home could talk, this one would recount tales of fabulous parties; it would recall hosting dignitaries, and being at the center of community action. It would speak of its beginnings—its designer, Virginia architect Duncan Lee, its construction in 1918—and its renown as the finest example of Georgian Revival architecture in all of Virginia. It might speak wistfully of being home to Douglas Southall Freeman, newspaper editor and Pulitzer prize-winning historian, until his death in 1953, for those were among its prime years. A president—Dwight Eisenhower—and a poet—Robert Frost—have been among its guests. And now, with its purchase by Justin and Tanya French, a new era begins.

Justin is a developer who buys and then renovates historic properties. Tanya is the mother of a toddler boy and an infant girl, a full-time job that keeps her on her toes. Yet

(CONTINUED ON PAGE 32)

Tanya and Justin manage to be at the forefront of causes they believe in, so this home appealed to them at several levels. They were looking for a family-oriented home with spacious grounds where children could play and explore. They also entertain a lot. "It was important that this house accommodate large crowds for fund-raisers," says Justin, "but also be comfortable enough for the children." They found their perfect match in this historic home.

The years had been kind to the venerable old place, but the young family's tastes necessitated changes. With a preference for comfortable traditional furnishings, contemporary art, and lots of color, Tanya knew that the rooms, previously all painted white, wouldn't satisfy them for long.

When a friend mentioned the work of Richmond interior designer Suellen Gregory, Tanya was somewhat familiar with it already. It wasn't long before she and Gregory were poring over paint chips and swatch books, seeking to transform the sterile rooms into a more personal space.

RIGHT TREATED TO TONES OF GOLD AND BLACK, THE MASCULINE LIBRARY HAS BECOME HOMEOWNER JUSTIN FRENCH'S FAVORITE ROOM. CHESTERFIELD SOFAS HAVE NEW BLACK SEAT CUSHIONS, TO BREAK UP THE EXPANSE OF TANNED LEATHER.

They started with the walls in the entry, treating them to 12-inch-wide vertical stripes of creamy white and crisp white paint, darkened with glaze. This subtle treatment, plus the black and white marble floor, creates the backdrop for colorful artwork and a magnificent pair of custom-made settees. The broad space is a gathering spot for guests at larger parties, and it sometimes serves as a playroom on rainy days.

Gregory notes that Harrison Higgins, the designer of the settees and other pieces, lives in the area. "Justin and Tanya

LEFT HANDSOME MOLDINGS AND FLOOR-LENGTH SILK DRAPERIES EDGED WITH VELVET ADD DIGNITY AND ELEGANCE TO THE DINING ROOM. AT NIGHT, THE SILVER-LEAF CEILING AND LARGE MIRROR CREATE A WONDERLAND OF LIGHT, REFLECTING THE GLOW OF CANDLES AND A CRYSTAL-DRAPED CHANDELIER.

LEFT THE SOLARIUM,
WITH FRENCH DOORS
OR WINDOWS ON THREE
SIDES, IS A SUNNY SPOT
FOR THE FAMILY TO
GATHER. OUTDOOR VIEWS
INSPIRED A PAINTED SKY
ON THE CEILING, ECHOED
BY SOFT BLUE WALLS
AND IVORY UPHOLSTERY.
DARK-STAINED PILASTERS
ADD EVEN MORE INTEREST
TO THE ROOM BY
CREATING THE ILLUSION
OF OUTDOOR COLUMNS.

really felt committed to using local craftsmen, just like you would have years ago," she says.

Tanya preferred that the living room be formal, yet somewhat feminine. Gregory drew its colors from the lush fabric that hangs from gold-twist curtain rods—the same period-inspired fabric, she adds, that was used for costuming in the Broadway production of *Les Misérables*.

Gentle tones of café au lait, rose, and pale aqua, reinforced by an Oushak rug in similar shades, set off dark wood, upholstered pieces, and relatively childproof accessories. Gregory excels in adding designer touches; she embellished the draperies with smocking, trimmed the pillows with

LEFT THE BATH NEXT
TO THE BABY'S ROOM
SHARES THE NURSERY'S
ROSY THEME. THE FABRIC
SKIRT ON THE PERIOD
PORCELAIN SINK HIDES
STORAGE SPACE.

OPPOSITE THE
CENTERPIECE IN THE
NURSERY IS THE ROUND
BED DRESSED IN TINTS OF
PINK. PALE FRENCH-BLUE
DRAPERIES EMPHASIZE
THE WINDOWS. SHADES
PULL DOWN TO DARKEN
THE ROOM FOR NAPTIME.

pleated edging, and added covered buttons and pleated skirts
to newly upholstered pieces.

Tanya and Gregory went even further in the dining room,
creating a silver-leaf ceiling that comes into its own at
night with the glow of candlelight and a crystal chandelier.
Draperies are pewter-color silk trimmed with velvet in a
darker shade. Antique pieces hug the walls of the large room,
and around the table, reproduction chairs mix comfortably
with others wearing slipcovers.

LEFT THE STURDY IRON POT RACK, MADE BY LOCAL ARTISANS GAVIN AND TY JARRARD, HANGS ABOVE THE ISLAND. THE PROFESSIONAL RANGE AND AMPLE GRANITE COUNTERTOPS ARE HANDY WHEN THE FRENCHES ENTERTAIN.

ABOVE ORIGINAL TO THE HOUSE, THE ORNATE RADIATOR WITH A BUILT-IN WARMING CABINET WAS MOVED TO THE KITCHEN DURING REMODELING.

Any young family needs plenty of casual space as well as "grown-up" areas. The Frenches spend a lot of time in the solarium, a sun-filled room where children can play and parents can try to read. Comfortable seating in creams and peaceful shades of blue beckons the family to sit and gaze upward at their favorite touch, the ceiling, which is painted to look like the sky.

Other rooms reflect those who use them most: Baby Chloe's room is an angelic vision in pink and white; Justin's library is a masculine lair of leather with black and gold. The totally renovated kitchen, known for producing an occasional cookie or two, is a favorite with Tanya and her son, Griffin. "We knew this house was home the minute we saw it," says Tanya. "We love pretty things—beautiful art and great furniture. We'll be able to share it with our kids. This is the home they will grow up in, and I love that."

# Gracious Manor

## This elegant home is a happy blend of venerable tradition and Southern grace.

LEFT IN THE DINING ROOM, A GILT-FRAMED MIRROR, PORCELAIN, AND CRYSTAL COMPLEMENT THE 200-YEAR-OLD SCOTTISH SIDEBOARD.

OPPOSITE LOCALLY FORGED SCROLLING IRONWORK FOR THE STAIRCASE RAILING WAS INSPIRED BY A DESIGN FOUND IN NEW ORLEANS.

Designing a home requires much more than putting pencil to paper and drawing something lovely. It takes months of thought, intensive trial and error, perseverance, and the skills of a psychologist to determine whether what the clients say they want is what they really want or need. It's fortunate when the architect's clients know what they would like but allow the architect to interpret their vision. And the client is indeed lucky if he has an architect who can translate the vision into reality, pulling together a home that not only suits the clients but exceeds their expectations.

Bulent Baydar, with the firm of Harrison Design Associates in Atlanta, was the principal architect of this appealing Tudor-style home in Chattanooga, Tennessee. Working with his clients, he did the mental homework that enabled him to create a plan ideally suited to its location and to the owners. Success came from Baydar's strong desire to reflect, as closely as possible, his clients' family and gracious attitudes in a structure of mere wood and stone.

The South has a special affinity for English and French architectural traditions, and the neighborhood where this

OPPOSITE THIS DISTINCTIVE BACK-WRAP STAIRCASE HAS A HANDWROUGHT RAILING THAT TIES IN WITH IRONWORK ON THE DOUBLE FRONT DOORS. HONED LIMESTONE FLOORING HAS INSERTS OF DARKER STONE.

ABOVE MIXING BRICK WITH STONE AND A SLATE ROOF GIVES THIS TENNESSEE HOME THE LOOK OF AN ENGLISH COUNTRY MANOR THAT HAS BEEN ENLARGED OVER THE YEARS.

house was built had fine examples of both. Baydar and his clients settled on a modified English Tudor style, quite formal with a facade combining handmade brick, cut stone, cast-stone eave corbels, a multicolor slate roof, and groupings of tall casement windows. The roof has numerous gables, and wooden doors with windows make the garage reminiscent of a carriage house. "It's a playful take on an English Tudor," Baydar says. "The materials and the way the roof rambles are still indicative of the style, but it's more contemporary."

Inside, rooms are spacious but not so large that they seem grandiose. "The homeowners appreciate simplicity, so the house is not overstated," says Baydar.

Indeed, in mirroring his clients, he added elegance while avoiding pretentiousness, focusing instead on creating a feeling of quality in even the smallest details. This is evident from the first step inside; the front doors open to an intimate

ABOVE GEOMETRIC SHAPES JOIN STYLIZED FLOWERS AND ACANTHUS LEAVES ON THE CARVED STONE MANTEL.

RIGHT A BARREL-VAULTED CEILING IS ONE OF THE HIGHLIGHTS OF THE LIVING ROOM. FLUSH LIMESTONE TILES CREATE THE ILLUSION THAT THE FIREPLACE WALL IS ONE SOLID STONE.

OPPOSITE IN THE DINING ROOM CHIPPENDALE CHAIRS SET A FORMAL MOOD, MADE EVEN MORE LOVELY BY A GILDED MIRROR, A 200-YEAR-OLD CHANDELIER, AND ANTIQUE CHINESE PORCELAIN IN THE FAMILLE ROSE STYLE.

RIGHT THE HIGH CEILING IN THE KITCHEN ALLOWS FOR EXTRA-TALL CABINETS IN A MELLOW GOLD STAIN WITH EGG-AND-DART MOLDING.

vestibule of normal ceiling height. Guests have a chance to greet and be greeted before stepping into the lofty hall with its curving walls and staircase. The flooring is limestone, continuing the stonework from outside. "It's a way to introduce the house in a series of steps," Baydar notes.

While the house is designed to look as though it's only a story-and-a-half, the back opens up to follow the slope of the property. Tall windows and towering arches take advantage of Chattanooga's spectacular views, yet as Baydar says, "From the front, it doesn't read as a two-story house."

The clients' family includes two active teenagers, whose friends find the house as welcoming as guests at a formal dinner party do. Partly this is because the home is decorated in an understated and entirely livable way, with a mix of antiques and new pieces, soft neutrals, and artwork that finds an echo in nearby accent colors.

The design team included interior designer Susan Young and kitchen designer Mary Kathryn Calonje. They worked with Baydar as they devised color palettes and chose furnishings that would enhance the 5,650-square-foot home. "This is a dream come true,"

OPPOSITE THE DEN, WITH ITS DEEP-STAINED WALNUT WOODWORK, HAS A MASCULINE DISPOSITION. ITS OVERSIZE OTTOMAN, GENEROUSLY FRINGED, SERVES AS A FIRESIDE BENCH, A FOOTREST, AND A COFFEE TABLE.

ABOVE THE LOGGIA IS A FAVORITE SPOT TO GATHER FOR COOKOUTS ON THE GRILL OR DRINKS BY THE LARGE STONE FIREPLACE ON COOL FALL EVENINGS. ARCHES SOAR TO 11 FEET, OFFERING A VIEW OF THE SPACIOUS GARDENS BEYOND.

says Young, "to start from scratch." She shopped mainly in the Chattanooga and Atlanta areas to find pieces for the house, because the homeowners brought very little of their previous furniture. The mid-South, settled primarily by the Scotch-Irish and English, abounds in antiques from Great Britain, and Atlanta is a world-class design center. Her finds included the 200-year-old sideboard in the dining room and the contemporary mirrored coffee table in the living room.

Young chose colors from the clients' paintings to add spice and liven up the palette. Gold, tangerine, and celadon are the predominant accents. "The homeowners love artwork, and

that was a great place to start for us," she says. A landscape painting above the living room fireplace ushers in gold, red, and orange. In the master bedroom, a cooler palette of ice blue, celadon, taupe, and off-white also comes from artwork.

The kitchen is warm and inviting with glazed paneled cabinets, faux-marble walls, and a backsplash made with small squares of polished marble. Granite countertops have an ogee edge with carved corbels adding traditional support.

"This whole project was a project of trust," Young says. "The homeowners trusted that this would be a livable, comfortable home, as well as beautiful." The house fulfills the promise—because its designers looked to the owners for their inspiration.

ABOVE Drawing its gentle color from Chinese pottery in the master bath, celadon accents the silver-foil wallpaper. The curving vanity evokes glamour worthy of a movie star.

RIGHT Spiraling bedposts and gilded furniture add drama to the master bedroom. Pleated edgings lend a designer touch to the draperies and valance.

53

# Georgian Influence

OVERLOOKING A PASTORAL SCENE IN MARYLAND, THIS HOME LOOKS CENTURIES OLD. SURPRISINGLY, IT'S ALMOST NEW.

LEFT A NEW WING CHAIR BLENDS FRENCH AND ENGLISH ELEMENTS FOR A FRESH INTERPRETATION OF TRADITIONAL STYLE.

OPPOSITE VISIBLE THROUGH THE PALLADIAN-INSPIRED ARCH, A GRACIOUS STAIRCASE IS THE DOMINANT FEATURE IN THE HALL THAT RUNS FROM FRONT DOOR TO BACK DOOR. THIS CENTRAL HALL IS CHARACTERISTIC OF MOST FINE GEORGIAN HOMES.

There are many ways for the "bloodlines" of historic homes to influence today's designs. Some recently built homes are like distant relatives, bearing a faint genetic resemblance, perhaps in the entry or roofline, to an architectural forebear. Others have lost any semblance of familiar tradition, incorporating a hodgepodge of other stylistic influences. Still others celebrate their architectural origins by adapting every appropriate detail as their own. This is one of them.

Built on an acreage in Maryland, the structure is of recent vintage. Architectural designer Caroline Boutté came as close in spirit to an 18th-century Georgian home as anyone could while suiting it to modern sensibilities.

She based the 5,860-square-foot floor plan on what she calls a "house-with-hyphens" style, paying homage to historic Georgian homes. In the 18th century, the original central block had two rooms upstairs and two rooms downstairs, divided by a center hall. A passageway (the hyphens) on each side connected the main block to single-story additions.

Boutté adapted the plan to a family home with a garage at each end, separating them from the house with hyphens,

OPPOSITE IN THE LIVING ROOM, GILDED CORNICES, DENTIL CROWN MOLDINGS, AND A BROKEN PEDIMENT ARE HALLMARKS OF GEORGIAN DESIGN. AN AUBUSSON RUG ANCHORS THE FURNITURE GROUPING.

ABOVE A CURVING DRIVE WINDS ITS WAY TOWARD THE FRONT OF THE HOME. CHIMNEYS WERE BUILT WITH AN OPEN ARCH TO KEEP THEM FROM APPEARING TOO HEAVY.

# GEORGIAN INFLUENCE

each composed of a hallway and a bath. The first floor still has four rooms and a spacious entry. One of those rooms is a large kitchen—a feature unheard of 250 years ago, when such rooms were often not even attached to the house, for fear of fire. Upstairs, four bedrooms, an enormous walk-in closet, baths, and an open stairwell fill out the floor plan. Bowing to the homeowners' needs, Boutté designed the rear of the house with an office tucked into a corner, a utility room close to the kitchen, and a workshop behind one garage.

A historically inspired floor plan, however, isn't enough to qualify a home as a Georgian Revival structure. The details that go into both exterior and interior finishing are truly what set such houses apart. They should mimic, as closely as possible, well-known models of the original style.

Outside, this home has rough-cast bricks to mimic handmade bricks, and they're laid in a Flemish bond pattern, alternating a whole brick with a half brick in every row. White trim, dentil moldings, 8-over-8- or 12-over-12 pane double-hung windows, and broad steps leading up to the doors are details typical of the Georgian Period.

OPPOSITE THE GOLDEN YELLOW COLOR ON THE DINING ROOM WALLS IS A SHADE OFTEN USED IN 18TH-CENTURY HOMES. TRADITIONAL WHITE MOLDING AND DARK WOOD FURNITURE ACCENT THE VIVID HUE.

Inside, all public rooms have elaborately built-up moldings that set off their classic proportions and high ceilings. In adjoining rooms not separated by a door, the common wall is double-thick with a paneled, arched opening for access. Walnut floors add weight underfoot to balance the interest above eye level.

Interior designer Arlene Critzos easily fell in step with Boutté's concept of authenticity, dressing the rooms in admirable Georgian style. In the living room, the fireplace, topped with a broken-pediment overmantel, is based on a similar one in the homeowners' previous home. It serves as the focal point in the room, flanked by a pair of wing chairs with carved and gilded frames. Because the family uses the room primarily for entertaining, Critzos chose furniture with comfortably plump upholstery, adding inlaid marble-top tables and a glass-top coffee table (a rare, more contemporary reference). Underneath, an Aubusson rug in pale yellow and rose pulls together all the colors in the room. The pale butter yellow walls are painted in a shade very close to the creamy shades found in Colonial Williamsburg.

A separate dining room was, of course, de rigueur in the days when George was king of England (there were actually four Georges, all kings, in successive generations). This room is

# Georgian Influence

LEFT A BATH OFF THE STUDY SHARES THE SAME RICH MARBLE AND HANDSOME COLORS. THE BATH'S PORTHOLE WINDOW IS ONE OF THREE IN THE HOUSE.

OPPOSITE THE STUDY, WITH RICH HAND-RUBBED LEATHER AND VELVET UPHOLSTERY, HAS WARM CHERRY PANELING. ACCESSORIES WITH A NAUTICAL OR HUNTING THEME CREATE A CLUBLIKE ATMOSPHERE.

also painted yellow, with a carved fireplace, dentil moldings, a crystal chandelier, and a massive table with Hepplewhite chairs. In a nod to the pastimes of 18th-century country gentlemen, the room has paintings of fox hunts and dogs.

When dinner is served in the dining room, the table setting is likely to be fine English bone china, silver, and cut-crystal stemware—elegant, antique, and authentic. Like most modern families, though, this one also needed a casual space to relax and enjoy its meals. The designers obliged with a spacious and casual kitchen/family room. Here, the family can gather in an informal setting that is still compatible with the rest of the home in color, fabrics, and materials.

Upstairs, the master suite has an elegant serenity. Like the other private rooms, it has simpler moldings and softer colors than the public areas downstairs. Shades of pale taupe and cream are restful for sleeping; they're also attractive in daylight, when the bedroom is used as a sitting room. Windows have swags and cornices over lined draperies; Critzos echoed the treatment in the adjoining marble bath, using only an unlined fabric swag on gilded tiebacks.

This home revels in its historic roots, and its Georgian detail is remarkable. Yet it manages to accommodate the needs of modern living, proving that a historical home can be both stylish and practical.

OPPOSITE THE MASTER BEDROOM IS A COMFORTABLE MIX OF NEUTRAL FABRICS, DEEP PILE CARPET, AND DRAMATIC WINDOW TREATMENTS. THE TRIMWORK IS SIMPLE YET ELEGANT IN THIS AND OTHER UPSTAIRS ROOMS— ONLY A CHAIR RAIL AND CROWN MOLDING.

ABOVE PINK MARBLE IS A LUXURIOUS CHOICE FOR THE MASTER BATH. THE WINDOW SCARF IS A SIMPLER ECHO OF THE DRAPERY TREATMENT IN THE BEDROOM.

# Cultural Tango

An English-born wife and a Cuban-born husband combine their passions in a California home where tradition dances to a Latin rhythm.

LEFT Evoking images of old Havana, a graceful window with a bombé ironwork balcony overlooks the courtyard.

OPPOSITE Massive front doors open into a 24-foot-tall entry with a Latin-inspired balcony. Inside, yellow damask walls and a limestone and marble floor evoke English inspiration.

LEFT WITH ITS DISTINCTLY SPANISH-STYLE ARCHITECTURE SET AMID LAVISH LANDSCAPING, THE EXTERIOR OF THE REYES HOME FEATURES STUCCO, WROUGHT IRON, AND ARCHED OPENINGS.

PAGES 70–71 WITH A NOD TOWARD GEORGIAN ENGLAND, MOLDINGS AND BLUE-AND-WHITE PORCELAIN SET A TRADITIONAL TONE IN THE LIVING ROOM.

Some couples would have given up in frustration at the challenge of combining two completely different tastes under one roof. Others would have settled for bland, passionless compromises that left neither person happy. Not so with English-born Vanessa and Cuban-born Greg Reyes, who danced into the complicated project with the give-and-take attitude of a longtime couple and created a Southern California home that reflects both of their personalities. Although it wasn't easy, both agree that it was enjoyable. "Everyone says how difficult building a house is," Vanessa says, "but we had tremendous fun."

Vanessa remembers going to visit her grandparents' home in England, and early on, she developed a penchant for formal mahogany furniture, Georgian architecture, and for blue-and-white porcelain. Greg favors Caribbean colors, vibrant oil paintings, and a (CONTINUED ON PAGE 72)

# Cultural Tango

RIGHT JEWEL-TONE
COLORS, INCLUDING
BLUE ON THE DRAMATIC
PAINTED PANELING,
APPEAL TO THE LATIN
TASTES OF HOMEOWNER
GREG REYES. THE
EARLY 19TH-CENTURY
PORCELAIN AND SILVER
ARE HEIRLOOMS FROM
HIS WIFE'S STAUNCHLY
BRITISH SIDE OF
THE FAMILY.

relaxed approach to decorating. Though their differences were apparent, the couple agreed to press ahead and look for common ground.

It all started in Greg and Vanessa's former home, a dark, one-story structure with little to recommend it. "One day, I said to my husband, 'I'd love to have a view,' " says Vanessa. "That started the ball rolling."

Finding a building site that was high on a hill with a 300-degree ocean view was an amazing stroke of luck, and architect Roy Asaro decided to capitalize on it. He hauled

(CONTINUED ON PAGE 76)

OPPOSITE YELLOW GLAZE HIGHLIGHTS THE WHITE CABINET DOORS AND WARMS UP THE KITCHEN. DECORATIVE CORBELS SUPPORT THE THICK MARBLE BREAKFAST BAR.

RIGHT THE BUTLER'S PANTRY IS THE STAGING AREA FOR ENTERTAINING. CEILING-HEIGHT CABINETS PROVIDE STORAGE FOR DISHES, GLASSWARE, AND VANESSA'S CHERISHED CHINESE EXPORT PORCELAIN. WARMING DRAWERS IN THE BASE CABINETS HOLD FOOD AT SERVING TEMPERATURE.

in tons of fill-dirt, not stopping until the building foundation was 4 feet higher. "Every foot we got in height increased the view tremendously," Asaro says. About the design of the house, he says, "It's a bat-wing U shape that kinks back and forth." There are views from nearly every room.

Working with the couple's preferences in the context of Spanish-settled California, he drew up a plan that leaned heavily toward Greg's side—at least on the exterior. Stucco walls, a Mission-style roof, wrought iron, balconies, fountains, and arches all suited a home with Hispanic flavor. Here, though, it deviated, with enough symmetrical features and moldings inside to thrill Vanessa—especially when she saw the authentic English conservatory at the back.

RIGHT Tucked between the kitchen and the conservatory, the breakfast nook is casually decked out in sunny yellow and blue. Mellow wood in rustic-style furniture and a random-plank floor add warmth as well.

LEFT In a bow to English preferences for pattern, the master bedroom mixes a bird print, checks, and plaid, all in blue tempered by white.

RIGHT The spacious walk-in closet keeps clothes dust-free inside 10-foot-tall cabinets with glass doors. An island of drawers takes the place of a dresser.

PAGE 80 The soaring conservatory, imported from England, serves as an extra dining area. Adjustable shades at the top control the bright sunshine.

PAGE 81 With walls of glass and doors leading outside, the teal blue English conservatory acts as a visual bridge between the house and terrace.

"We have a lot of Georgian furniture, and it suits a more formal space," Vanessa says. "I wanted an interior where I could show off those things to maximum effect." Teaming with interior designer Elizabeth Thiele Barkett, she set out to create a "veddy, veddy proper" setting. By this time her furnishings included a collection of inherited English porcelain, as well as the many blue-and-white pieces she had assembled over the years.

Barkett and Asaro organized the project by dividing the home into two main districts: formal and more casual. The living room, dining room, and entryway are traditional in every sense, with beautifully paneled and painted walls, oak-parquet or marble floors, shiny brass hardware, and the 18th- and 19th-century furniture—plus accoutrements such as antique oil paintings and porcelain—that Vanessa prefers. Barkett researched 18th-century Southern and English homes, looking in countless books for authentic details, adding egg and dart, dentils, and three-tiered crown moldings. (CONTINUED ON PAGE 83)

OPPOSITE A TILE-
ROOF PAVILION ECHOES
THE STYLE OF THE
MAIN HOUSE. WITH THE
WARM CLIMATE, THE
FAMILY OFTEN USES THIS
SPACE FOR DINING AND
ENTERTAINING FRIENDS.

ABOVE WEATHER-
RESISTANT FURNITURE,
A COZY FIREPLACE, A
PLASMA TV, AND HEATERS
IN THE RAFTERS ADD
YEAR-ROUND COMFORTS
TO THE OUTDOOR ROOM.

The more casual zone, including the kitchen and breakfast areas, has pecan-plank flooring, oil-rubbed bronze hardware, stained moldings, and a simpler, brighter mix of gingham and toile fabrics with sturdy furniture. Its sunny disposition greatly appeals to Greg and the children. And everyone loves the conservatory. "Our idea was to have an elegant house, but we also wanted a home," Vanessa says.

The color blue ties the two cultures—English and Cuban—together. As the blue dances from room to room, only the accents vary. Blue with white leads off, then does a side-step with green and raspberry in the dining room, finishing with a triple-spin of yellow in the formal living room, entry, and the casual kitchen area.

Partners Vanessa and Greg love it. "We both put our heart and soul into this house," Vanessa says. "We were completely involved in everything. This was not going to be a house where other people made all the decisions." And, she adds, "Everything exceeded our wildest dreams."

# 2 Rooted in History

# Style Above the City

AFTER MOVING FROM THEIR OLD HOME, A PAIR OF EMPTY NESTERS OPT FOR A CHANGE OF STYLE AS WELL AS SCENERY.

LEFT ANTIQUES, WARM COLORS, AND POLISHED WOOD GIVE THE APARTMENT AN INTIMATE FEELING. BEYOND THE WINDOWS LIES A SPECTACULAR VIEW OF BOSTON.

OPPOSITE WITH CUSTOM STAINED AND PAINTED FLOORS, PAPER-BACKED FABRIC WALLS, AND ELEGANT MOLDINGS, THE ENTRY OFFERS A STUNNING FIRST IMPRESSION OF NANCY AND JOE SERAFINI'S NEW HOME.

LEFT THAT CLASSIC
BRITISH FAVORITE—A
TUFTED CHESTERFIELD
SOFA—OFFERS A
COMFORTABLE CHOICE
FOR SEATING IN THE
LIVING ROOM. STRIPED
TAFFETA PANELS IN GOLD
AND DEEP RED HAVE
EXTRA-TALL HEADERS
AND ANTIQUE BRONZE
TIEBACKS. INTRICATE
BEADED PILLOWS FROM
ENGLAND ECHO TWINING
MOTIFS IN THE RUG.

Living in the city wasn't something that Nancy and Joe Serafini set out to do. They were happily ensconced in their Wellesley, Massachusetts, home of 20 years—where they had brought up two children—when they first saw the apartment. It is a 3,400-square-foot space in a 10-story 1929 building in the choice Back Bay area of Boston, and the two were instantly entranced.

With windows on all four sides, the spacious seventh-floor apartment has panoramic views of the Charles River and the Boston skyline. Inside, the rooms are large and have the substantial character that buildings of the early 1900s so often possess. "Moving into Boston wasn't a deliberate, pre-planned decision on our part," Nancy says. "We just liked the apartment and we bought it."

Their former home was decorated in an upscale country style with cheerful yellows, blues, and reds. Nancy, an interior

LEFT NANCY SERAFINI ADDED MORE BOOKCASES IN JOE'S STUDY, THEN FINISHED THE WALLS AND WOODWORK IN THE RICH BURGUNDY THAT IS HIS FAVORITE SHADE.

RIGHT THE LIVING ROOM HAS NEWLY REJUVENATED WALNUT PANELING. THE 26-FOOT-LONG ROOM SHOWCASES THREE SEPARATE SITTING AREAS, EACH ANCHORED BY ONE LARGE FURNITURE PIECE.

designer known for her ability to combine colors into striking palettes, realized that she'd need to rethink some of her choices to create the sophisticated city home she envisioned. But first, the apartment needed a lot of work.

"I believe the architecture must be right before the decorating begins," Nancy says. She hired architect Mark Howland to reconfigure the floor plan, asking him to make some rooms larger and reallocate the space in others. As empty nesters, the Serafinis needed fewer bedrooms, so one was converted to a study for Joe, who is an attorney. A hodgepodge arrangement that included another bedroom, a cedar closet, two servant's rooms, and a bath became a master suite that better suits the family. "The master suite is an architectural triumph," Nancy says, exclaiming over the transformation.

Despite its vintage character, the apartment needed a bit more polish. Deep crown molding now graces the walls of all the rooms. When old floor coverings were removed, wooden floors came to light and were restored to their original appearance. In the entry, an oak floor wears

OPPOSITE DINING ROOM
CHAIRS WEAR FABRIC
BASED ON A MEDIEVAL
TAPESTRY SCENE:
HINDS—A TYPE OF DEER—
SCAMPER THROUGH
STYLIZED LEAVES.
BAMBOO SHADES PICK
UP THE FABRIC'S TONES.

LEFT THE TEXTURED
WALLCOVERING IS A
JACOBEAN-DESIGN
CREWEL FABRIC,
EMBROIDERED IN WOOL
ON A COTTON GROUND
AND FIXED TO PAPER
BACKING. IT HELPS
MUFFLE CITY SOUNDS.

a pattern of light- and dark-stained squares; painted stars at intersections give a preview of the red used in other rooms. Opulent golds, mossy greens, and the mix of reds, all leaning toward rose or burgundy, create a burnished palette appropriate to the city setting.

Nancy lavished attention on the walls by choosing paper-backed fabrics instead of wallpaper; she covered the entry in a golden botanical toile. Then, for the dining room, she found an embroidered crewel in gold, brown, and green that adds texture, warmth, and richness. The fabric also absorbs sound so the room feels quiet and intimate.

The living room had lovely walnut paneling that Nancy restored to its former glory. Friends were so impressed by its improved appearance that they urged Nancy to give the same treatment to Joe's study. Instead, Nancy honored Joe's desire for a burgundy red room. "It was the only thing he requested during the whole remodeling," she says.

It took a year to complete the remodeling process and then another year of intensive decorating to make the apartment home. Many of the Serafinis' former furnishings were

LEFT TILES WITH A DAINTY GREEN, BROWN, BLUE, AND GOLD MOTIF FORM A FIREPLACE SURROUND THAT LOOKS DELICATE DESPITE ITS AMPLE SIZE.

RIGHT WITH CASUAL FABRICS OF YELLOW AND DUSTY RED, THE FAMILY ROOM BEARS THE CLOSEST RESEMBLANCE TO THE SERAFINIS' COUNTRY-STYLE FORMER HOME.

PAGES 96–97 BURGUNDY RED FLOWS THROUGH EVERY ROOM; THE MASTER BEDROOM IS NO EXCEPTION. HERE, LARGE DOSES OF CREAMY WHITE OFFSET THE VISUAL WEIGHT OF THE COLOR, WHILE A MIX OF FABRICS LOOSENS UP THE STYLE. THE WATERCOLOR PAINTINGS ABOVE THE BED WERE JOE'S GIFT TO NANCY ON HER BIRTHDAY.

too informal for their new home, so Nancy kept only their favorite pieces and a few heirlooms, such as the camelback sofa that had belonged to Joe's mother. She filled the rooms with gleaming wood and plump upholstered pieces chosen for both looks and comfort. Only in the family room did she revert to her previous color scheme, yet even here, country elements morph into a more sophisticated character.

The furniture is a happy blend of antiques, such as an 1850 mahogany sideboard, and antique look-alikes, such as the new Regency-style dining room table. A smattering of Asian treasures add a global accent. Nancy long ago discovered that it doesn't matter what the original purpose of a piece was; if it works well as something else, she'll use it. A case in point is the handpainted leather box serving as a coffee table in the family room. (CONTINUED ON PAGE 99)

AMERICAN FOLK

Bedrooms

Decorating Secrets

Living with DOGS

SENSATIONAL BOUQUETS

Pattern, too, is a major tool in Nancy's overhauling of the apartment. She favors a mix of large-scale florals, smaller checks, narrow stripes, and plenty of solids for relief. She's especially fond of intertwining-vine motifs, such as the one that appears in the living room rug—golden tendrils in a field of claret. Wallcoverings and upholstery fabrics reflect these preferences, and Nancy punctuates the look by tossing in pillows with intricate hand-applied beading or needlework.

Now that Nancy has finished working on their home, she and Joe can relax a bit and get back to normal activities. There are some differences, though. Joe is now within walking distance of work, and Nancy is much closer to the Boston Children's Hospital, her favorite charity. They still entertain, the children come to visit and stay overnight, and life goes on. The Serafinis' new apartment feels like home now, although they may never grow used to seeing one feature: Every time they pause at a window, they feel a thrill. As their friends so frequently say, "Oh, just look at those views."

# Exuberant Tastes

Color and pattern go hand in hand. That's the consensus of design firm Diamond Baratta, whose love for both is a way of life.

LEFT THE YOUNGEST RESIDENT'S PET GUINEA PIG OFTEN EATS A CARROT WHILE POLITELY SITTING UP IN AN ANTIQUE WALNUT HIGH CHAIR.

OPPOSITE PATTERN ON PATTERN IS AN APPEALING LOOK FOR THOSE WHO CRAVE VISUAL EXCITEMENT. A DELIGHTFUL LITTLE PAPIER-MÂCHÉ TABLE IS A PERFECT CHOICE AGAINST THE VIBRANT RUG.

If a collector meets a designer who shares a taste for color and copious patterns, the results are likely to be exciting. There's a caution, though. If a family of collectors meets two such designers and lets them take the lead, the result could be color cacophony—unless the project is conducted with the utmost skill.

New York interior designers William Diamond and Anthony Baratta specialize in wielding control over pattern, color, and collections. Indeed, they thrive on the mix. Taking a multi-level approach to traditional style, they add paint to painted surface, fabric to fabric, pattern to pattern, and detail to detail until they achieve a happily, if precariously, layered result.

The two designers, who have had a partnership called Diamond Baratta for 25 years, take their cue from such industry greats as the late Sister Parish, who firmly believed that chintz, rag rugs, painted furniture and floors, and bold color everywhere are the only way to go—as long as the client likes it. The client in this particular home likes it so much that she commissioned Diamond and Baratta to do her entire home, a 5,000-square-foot "cottage"

OPPOSITE DELFT TILE ADORNS A 19TH-CENTURY FIREPLACE IN THE FAMILY ROOM ADDITION. HORIZONTAL SIDING IS AN INFORMAL WALL SURFACE.

ABOVE POTTERY, PATTERN, AND PAINTED FURNITURE COMBINE TO CREATE A COLOR-FILLED ROOM THAT SOARS TO NEW HEIGHTS.

LEFT SCALLOPED
EDGING ON THE TOILE
DRAPERY IS A BOW TO
WINDOW TREATMENTS
BY THE LATE—AND NOW
LEGENDARY—INTERIOR
DESIGNER SISTER PARISH,
WHO WAS ALSO KNOWN
FOR HER LOVE
OF PATTERN.

OPPOSITE AGAIN
AGREEING WITH ICON
SISTER PARISH, WHO
SAID, "THIS IS THE
ONLY WAY YOU CAN DO
THESE BIG PALLADIAN
WINDOWS," DIAMOND
AND BARATTA CHOSE
SYMMETRICAL DRAPING
IN THE FAMILY ROOM. A
LARGE RASPBERRY SOFA,
PLUMPED WITH PILLOWS,
ANCHORS THE SEATING.

now expanded to 14,000 square feet. The designers, knowing what was ahead, prepared themselves for a wild ride.

Built in the 1930s, the home has a white clapboard exterior, black shutters, and a simple front porch. The unassuming exterior gives no hint of the colorful exuberance within. Vernacular furnishings seem heightened, stretching to the utmost limits of their style by means of color or scale. Rag rugs, most often seen in pale colors, show up in vivid cobalt blue and hot pink. Chintz, which in many homes would be the only print in the room, is here only one of many patterned fabrics. A small motif gleaned from an antique textile is magnified and painted 10 times its original size to decorate a piece of furniture. These bold choices please both the client and the designers because they make the large home seem more cozy. (CONTINUED ON PAGE 109)

OPPOSITE THE RUSTIC
FRONT DOOR, COMPLETE
WITH ITS ORIGINAL LOCKS
AND HARDWARE, DATES
TO THE ORIGINAL LARGE
1930S "COTTAGE."

RIGHT NEOCLASSICAL
MOLDINGS, ENGLISH
ACCESSORIES, AND
LARGE-SCALE PATTERNED
WALLPAPER—USUALLY
FLORALS OR TOILE—ARE
CONSTANTS THROUGHOUT
THE HOME. FURNITURE IS
A MIX OF COMFORTABLE
UPHOLSTERED PIECES
AND PERIOD ANTIQUES.

OPPOSITE LIKE AN
ENGLISH COUNTRY
GARDEN GROWING WILD,
FLOWERS SPRING UP
EVERYWHERE IN THE
COZY BREAKFAST ROOM.
RED PLAID CUSHIONS
INTRODUCE A BRIGHT
NOTE AROUND THE
GEORGIAN TABLE,
PICKING UP THEIR SHADE
FROM THE ENGLISH
NEEDLEPOINT RUG.

RIGHT IN A HARMONIOUS
DISPLAY OF PATTERN ON
PATTERN, STAFFORDSHIRE
POTTERY HOLDS ITS
OWN AGAINST TOILE
WALLPAPER. THE WELSH
DRESSER SERVES AS A
FRAME FOR THE POTTERY.

Diamond says, "Our client has exquisite tastes. She loves what she loves, and she doesn't care what goes in and out of style." Baratta adds, "She could look at chintz fabric every day. We love her."

When they choose fabrics, the two designers have an unerring eye for scale, carefully balancing small, medium, and large prints to establish a visual dynamic rather than have prints too close in size fighting for dominance. When considering scale, Diamond and Baratta also factor in wallpaper, rugs, and any other element that covers a large surface. Toile patterns, for instance, are often large-scale, because they have scenic subjects; so when using a toile wallpaper, the designers would likely go with a check, stripe, or smaller flower print for draperies or upholstered furniture rather than introducing another large-scale element. The art of the mix sometimes depends on color, though.

It's as important to establish a workable palette in each room as it is to choose compatible prints. Drawing the color from their client's extensive collection of Staffordshire pottery, Diamond and Baratta use blue as a constant in most of the rooms to pull the whole scheme together. That color family, though, ranges from palest blue in the master suite to a rousing blue that could wake up a carpet.

RIGHT WALLPAPER FORMS A ROSE-COVERED BOWER FOR THE VANITY IN THE BATH. THE 19TH-CENTURY ENGLISH DRESSING TABLE NOW HAS PAINTED FLOWERS, A NEW MARBLE TOP, AND PLUMBING FIXTURES FOR 21ST-CENTURY FUNCTION.

OPPOSITE UBIQUITOUS BLUE AND WHITE, THE HOMEOWNER'S FAVORITE PALETTE, FINDS ITS WAY TO THE UPSTAIRS LANDING. A NEEDLEPOINT RUNNER AND PASTORAL TOILE WALLPAPER ARE THE MAIN COLOR SOURCES, ECHOED BY BLUE-MATTED CURRIER & IVES PRINTS AND THE FABRIC ON ANTIQUE ENGLISH CHAIRS.

The homeowner's collections do more than set up the color scheme—they are essential to the character of the home. Much of the artwork consists of authentic Currier & Ives prints, each one in an antique frame. It took Diamond and Baratta many months to come up with more than 200 frames of the right size and period.

Even though the homeowner already had an extensive collection of blue-and-white Staffordshire pottery, now displayed on a Welsh dresser in the breakfast room and on family room shelves, the designers felt that more was needed. "I'll never forget how we went into this shop in London," Baratta says. "Libra Antiques, off Kensington Church Road, is only 15 feet long and 7 feet wide, and it had 2,000 pieces of Staffordshire. We had a car and driver

outside, and for half a day, I kept running out, telling him 'Just another five minutes.' We bought out the shop."

The designers also took matters into their own hands when picking rugs for the home. Not finding what they were seeking, they designed custom rugs in Portuguese needlepoint. They were free to manipulate color and scale all they wanted, even taking an element from an 18th-century rug and enlarging it for their own version (see page 102), with certain changes. "We blew it up, added huge baskets of flowers, and recolored it, keeping the checkerboard and the ribbon," Baratta explains. Each square was designed with baskets of daffodils, roses, hydrangeas, tulips, and lilacs, mirroring the flowers in the homeowner's own garden.

RIGHT TUCKED INTO AN ARCHED NICHE CREATED WHEN THE CEILING WAS RAISED, THE PAINTED BED IS TOPPED WITH A CROWN OF GATHERED FABRIC. LARGE-SCALE WALLPAPER IN BLUE AND WHITE IS REINFORCED BY FLORAL FABRICS. RIBBONS, TOO, ARE A CONTINUING MOTIF, FOUND IN THE RUG AND CHINTZ-COVERED ARM CHAIRS. THE VICTORIAN BENCH IS TURNED WOOD WITH AN APPLIED PAPIER-MÂCHÉ FINISH.

LEFT A PAINTED TURNED-POST BED AND A EUROPEAN-INSPIRED TRUNK WITH HAND-PAINTED FLOWERS PLEASE THE YOUNG OCCUPANT OF THIS ROOM AND WILL STILL APPEAL TO HER AS SHE MATURES.

RIGHT THIS VICTORIAN "DOLLHOUSE," DESIGNED BY DIAMOND BARATTA, IS A CHARMING DISGUISE FOR THE STORAGE CLOSET BEHIND IT.

The designers did the same sort of personalizing with several wing chairs, covering each with a custom-made tartan in pink, blue, gray, green, white, and yellow. "I must have been Scottish in another life," says Diamond. "I invent clans for all of my clients because I love tartans so much." Lee Jofa has even launched the Diamond Baratta fabric collection. It features plaids, of course.

The play of pattern continues into the bedroom of the homeowner's daughter, who had an opportunity to share her own ideas with Diamond and Baratta. The three decided together on patterns in large, medium, and small, with woven rag rugs, a flowered bedspread, painted furniture, and an armoire modeled after a playhouse. "One pattern ignites the other," Diamond says. "Quintessential Sister Parish."

# Riverside
# Beauty

TAKING ON A CHALLENGE,
A DESIGNING COUPLE
TRANSFORMS THE
NEIGHBORHOOD PROBLEM
INTO A CHARMING AND
LIVABLE HOME.

LEFT REFLECTING THE
SUNNY ROOM, A CONVEX
MIRROR CREATES THE
ILLUSION OF A SMALL
PORTHOLE WINDOW.

OPPOSITE DINING
ROOM CHAIRS SPORT
LINEN SLIPCOVERS
EMBROIDERED WITH
THE HOMEOWNERS'
MONOGRAM. AN 18TH-
CENTURY ETCHED
MERCURY-GLASS
SCONCE HOLDS A PAIR
OF CANDLES.

OPPOSITE STANDING SENTINEL BY THE DOOR, A VENERABLE NEWEL POST HINTS AT THE HOWARDS' TASTES IN FURNISHINGS. LIKE MANY SOUTHERN HOMES, THIS ONE COMBINES ANTIQUES, WELL-MADE REPRODUCTIONS, AND LOCAL NATURAL MATERIALS. A DISPLAY OF LIVING PLANTS IN EVERY ROOM IS AN IMPORTANT ELEMENT OF THE "SOUTHERN LOOK."

Living by the shore of the St. Johns River has its advantages: The patient flow of the water tends to put a busy day in perspective. On a warm evening, there's a harmony of nature as birds settle in for the night and hundreds of fireflies decide to come courting. Out on the terrace, Jim and Phoebe Howard sit with their guests and then wander down to the pier to see the lights of downtown Jacksonville, Florida, in the distance.

Afterward, they linger around the mahogany dining room table, talking and occasionally glancing up to the crystal chandelier and sky blue ceiling. It's the kind of evening the couple hoped for when they decided to buy their home. "Whenever I think of this room," says Phoebe, "I think of it bathed in candlelight and filled with friends and laughter."

Few in their historic Ortega neighborhood could have imagined that the two-story 1910 house, which was on the market far too long because of structural problems and a poor floor plan, would have such a happy ending. Phoebe, the owner of a design and antiques shop, and Jim, an interior designer, saw past its deficiencies and envisioned its possibilities.

The two oversaw the transformation over a 10-month period, using Jim's plans to narrow the front hallway, put in a staircase custom-built in New Orleans, and raise low ceilings wherever possible. Outside, in keeping with other neighborhood homes, the couple relocated windows for symmetry, adding cedar shingles and a new entry with classically proportioned Doric columns. (CONTINUED ON PAGE 122)

PAGES 120–121 THE TUFTED ENGLISH NURSING CHAIR, SO NAMED BECAUSE IT'S LOW TO THE FLOOR FOR MINDING CHILDREN, WAS ONCE OWNED BY INTERIOR DESIGNER NANCY LANCASTER. DENTIL MOLDINGS ADD A PLEASINGLY FORMAL TOUCH AT THE CEILING, WHICH IS PAINTED PALE SKY BLUE.

LEFT DECORATIVE PAINTER BOB CHRISTIAN MIMICKED CYPRESS ON THE HALLWAY WALLS. AGAINST THIS PAINTED FACSIMILE, FRENCH ENGRAVINGS AND A GILDED ITALIAN MIRROR ACCENT THE GEORGE III DESK, CIRCA 1790.

OPPOSITE A HARMONY OF TEXTURES—VELVET, BROCADE, GRASS CLOTH, AND BAMBOO—CREATES A COMFORTABLE SETTING FOR FAMILY ROOM CONVERSATION. THE 19TH-CENTURY ENGLISH PINE MANTEL IS A HANDSOME FOCAL POINT.

While a student at Parsons School of Design, Jim had been impressed by the work of interior design icons Mark Hampton and Nancy Lancaster. When designing interiors for this home, Jim returned to the lessons he'd learned from them. From Hampton, he drew the concept of creating "teasers" by means of cased openings that allow a partial view into another, larger room. From Lancaster, a Virginia-born socialite who moved to England and became the grande dame of the English country style, he learned the importance of putting unpretentious livability first, blending items he and Phoebe love into a comfortable mix.

(CONTINUED ON PAGE 127)

LEFT MONOGRAMMED LINEN SLIPCOVERS ADORN THE DINING ROOM CHAIRS, SOFTENING THE FORMALITY OF FURNISHINGS THAT INCLUDE A SCOTTISH SIDEBOARD, CIRCA 1840.

BELOW INSPIRED BY ARRANGEMENTS OF THE 18TH CENTURY, A FEDERAL-STYLE CONVEX MIRROR CROWNS A SYMMETRICAL DISPLAY.

OPPOSITE A private sitting area in the master bedroom is a favorite spot to read or reflect. Textured fabrics add interest without detracting from the overall neutral color scheme.

RIGHT Restful in softest blue, a Swedish-inspired extra bedroom has embroidered linens, an upholstered headboard, and other amenities that offer homelike comfort to visiting guests.

Accordingly, his front hallway offers views of the living room, family room, and kitchen. Conversation groups have comfortable seating, table space, and enough light for reading.

The Howards chose a water-inspired palette of cool blues and greens with soft neutrals and brown accents, even painting the dining and living room ceilings blue. Phoebe explains, "I wanted to look out the window toward the river, take in the view, and then see the same colors inside." The colors are a perfect foil for antique furniture in polished mahogany and walnut, and they also highlight the collection of English and American landscape paintings. "We like the serene, familiar, and comfortable moods these paintings evoke," Jim says.

Once, when on a buying trip to England, they toured Lancaster's home and office. While there, they discovered that a piece of her furniture—an antique English nursing chair—was for sale, so they promptly bought it. Now that chair, with fabric unchanged, sits by their living room fireplace, surrounded by antiques, English boxes, J.M.W. Turner engravings, and other furnishings that would surely have her approval. "It's the only thing in the house that I wouldn't sell," says Jim. Guests often express amused doubts about the low-slung seat, but regardless of the chair, they feel comfortable in the ways that really matter. The gracious house by the river and its equally gracious owners take care of that.

# Designer's Choice

Noted designer Charles Spada prefers that his surroundings be a serene reflection of his design philosophy.

LEFT A CLASSIC MARBLE BUST IS EMBLEMATIC OF CHARLES' STRONG PREFERENCE FOR ANTIQUES. HE SAYS, "ANTIQUES ARE FOREVER."

OPPOSITE PUSS, CHARLES SPADA'S 2-YEAR-OLD CAT, HAS TAKEN OVER A FRENCH FOOTSTOOL THAT NOW SERVES AS HIS PERSONAL DAYBED.

The waterfront home of award-winning interior designer Charles Spada looks out over Boston Harbor. Like sun breaking through an early morning fog, its light-filled rooms envelop their occupants in quiet warmth. The home is comfortable, yet elegant. Only in looking closely does one realize how its elements work together to create an environment that promotes reflection and creativity.

Charles is a man who is good at many things; he is an artist who draws and paints, a student of architecture, a collector, a seller of antiques, a writer, and—not least—a designer with strong commitment to his craft. "You can make a painting that gives pleasure," he says, "but in design and decorating, you have a chance to create a universe that in itself is a total work of art."

He has devised for himself several such universes. He spends weekends in a tiny Connecticut Cape Cod built in

OPPOSITE AMID TRADITIONAL FURNITURE IN PALEST GRAYS, A GOLD-LEAF STAR MAKES AN EYE-CATCHING AND AMUSING TABLE BASE. GILDED ACCENTS ELSEWHERE CARRY THROUGH THE THEME.

ABOVE MIRRORED DOORS CREATE THE ILLUSION OF MORE SPACE AND REFLECT AN ANTIQUE GLOBE THAT IS CHARLES' FAVORITE POSSESSION.

LEFT GOLDEN FINIALS AND SILKEN TASSELS PLAY UP THE STYLING ON THE SOFA CHARLES DESIGNED. IT IS FASHIONED AFTER AN 18TH-CENTURY "KNOLE" SOFA WITH SIDES THAT FOLD DOWN FOR COMFORTABLE RECLINING.

RIGHT FRENCH DRAWINGS REFLECTED IN THE MIRROR AND ITALIAN ART FLANKING IT GAIN PROMINENCE IN THE MONOCHROMATIC ROOM.

1690, owns a pied-à-terre in Palm Beach, and is thinking of buying a place in Paris, the city that makes him feel most at home—but more exotic realms entice him too. And then, there's Boston, where he spends most of his time.

Those who know Charles have often heard him expound on his preference for spare window treatments that offer both light and privacy, bare wood floors with an occasional rug, and textured furnishings with neutral colors. His personal credo would likely read: Less is more. Spare is beautiful. Antiques are forever. His Boston condominium reflects all these tenets without seeming too sparse or in any way contrived. Instead, it is a gracious reflection of Charles' design philosophy.

"Most of my clients come to me for soft simplicity," Charles says. "There's never any nonsense that would make either a man or woman uncomfortable." To achieve such simplicity, he starts with color, or, more specifically, a lack of it. "I prefer an absence of color at home

because there's so much color all around us," he says. "A neutral palette enhances any display."

His favorite neutral is gray, a preference that began early. One of his career mentors was Morgan Fauth, whose home in New York was filled with French antiques in the palest-possible smoky gray. "I've never forgotten the 'oneness' of his living room," Charles says. "It took my breath away. Looking back, I recognize it had a great influence on my present work." He extends the "neutral" concept to any color, including red, as long as all tones have the same color value. The student now promotes the principle.

Charles also celebrates natural light. "I see no reason for too many objects in a light-filled room," he says. "But if you

(CONTINUED ON PAGE 139)

ABOVE THE DINING AREA HAS A WALL OF SHUTTERS FOR PRIVACY; THEY FURNISH AN EVER-MOVING PATTERN OF LIGHT DURING THE DAY.

RIGHT SIMPLE GILT FRAMES ENHANCE TRADITIONAL LANDSCAPE PAINTINGS. A FRENCH 19TH-CENTURY IRON UMBRELLA STAND HOLDS WALKING STICKS.

RIGHT ONE ANTIQUE
ACCENT—THE 19TH-
CENTURY FRENCH
TABLE THAT STILL WEARS
ITS ORIGINAL BLUE AND
GOLD PAINT—WAKES UP
THE COLOR SCHEME
IN THE GUEST ROOM.
A CUSTOM DAYBED
UPHOLSTERED IN A
SIMPLE PINSTRIPE
QUIETLY COMPLEMENTS
THE 19TH-CENTURY
ARTWORK ON THE
WALLS ABOVE.

have a room without good light, you're almost required to fill it wall to wall with possessions, to make it feel warm and inviting."

The high-rise condo was a bare-bones box when Charles bought it, but the quality of light was wonderful. "There was great potential in its simplicity," he says. "The space was so characterless." He launched into changing the surfaces, smoothing bumpy ceilings and adding wainscoting, chair rails, crown molding, and deep baseboards. He stained the wooden floors dark walnut and gave all the walls a combed finish—white paint over gray—framed with crisp white woodwork. With a bow to his mentor, Charles dressed almost all the furnishings in monochromatic gray. This is a perfect foil for finely drawn etchings, studio drawings, bucolic landscapes, and mirrors, all with gold-leaf frames.

Charles' irrepressible side can't be held down for long, though, so he indulges in some confident additions. Tiger-print chairs and a gilded-star table base jump out against the muted background. These masterly surprises, too, can take the breath away.

OPPOSITE TIGER-PRINT VELVET CHAIRS ADD A JOLT OF COLOR TO THE MASTER BEDROOM. SPADA DISPLAYS HIS PARENTS' WEDDING PHOTOS ON A PAINTED FRENCH WRITING DESK.

ABOVE A PAINTED LINEN CUPBOARD OFFERS STORAGE; A BENCH ACTS AS A BEDSIDE TABLE.

# Authentic Setting

Inspired by a love of all things Colonial, Georgia homeowners build a new home rooted in America's early history.

LEFT BRICK FLOORS AND PRIMITIVE FURNISHINGS ESTABLISH A CASUAL MOOD IN THE SUNROOM.

OPPOSITE WHILE THE SUNNY KITCHEN HAS EVERY MODERN CONVENIENCE, FEATURES SUCH AS THE PORCELAIN FARMHOUSE SINK, LARGE KNOBS, AND PERIOD ACCESSORIES ADD TO ITS "ANTIQUE" APPEAL.

When the history bug bites, there's little point in resisting. Ann and Mark Rogers should know, because for more than 15 years, they've traveled all over New England immersing themselves in the Colonial past. It's not an idle interest— they've visited historic towns, stayed in homes that have been around for generations, purchased period furniture, and learned everything they can about the architecture and gardens of the Colonial era.

An avid researcher, Ann has spent hours and hours poring over reference books and home magazines, trying to glean information. It's no wonder that when it came time to build their new home on St. Simons Island, Georgia, Ann and Mark picked a Colonial style.

Authenticity was paramount in their decision to build; with their knowledge, they could hardly have lived in the house otherwise. The only departure from the traditional architecture was their desire to have the interior be more light-filled than some of the homes they had visited. "The one negative about Colonials is they tend to be boxy and dark," Ann says. "I wanted more of an open feel."

OPPOSITE PERIOD DETAILS SUCH AS HEART PINE FLOORS, RAISED-PANEL WAINSCOTING, FLUTED PILASTERS, TURNED SPINDLES, AND DECORATIVE TREAD BRACKETS HEIGHTEN THE FEELING OF AUTHENTICITY IN THE HOME. THE OWNERS PURCHASED THE HIGH-BACK ANTIQUE SETTLE, CIRCA 1800, WHILE IN ENGLAND.

ABOVE LEFT INSPIRED BY COLONIAL GARDENS, THE FRONT GARDEN HAS BRICK WALKWAYS THAT MEANDER THROUGH THE PLANTING POCKETS.

ABOVE RIGHT THE NEWLY BUILT HOME IS AN AUTHENTIC COLONIAL, WITH 12-OVER-12 PANE WINDOWS, CLAPBOARD SIDING, AND A PICKET FENCE THAT ALLOWS A CLEAR VIEW FROM INSIDE.

Architect Larry Bryson obliged by creating an L-shape footprint for them, although the view from the street is a simple box shape with a picket fence and a boxwood garden. The additional wing takes advantage of a glorious view of the nearby lake surrounded by spreading live-oak trees. Bryson also positioned the stairway so the entry could be open to the second floor.

The entry provides a good introduction to the quality of the construction. Golden heart pine flooring, raised paneling and fluted columns painted white, and the gracious, extra-wide stairway announce the traditional character of the home. Six-panel doors and 12-over-12 pane windows are used throughout, reinforcing the Colonial style.

RIGHT CREAMY WHITE PANELING ENSURES THAT THE LIVING ROOM IS A LIGHT AND AIRY SPACE. GLAZED-COTTON CHINTZ, EVEN MORE POPULAR IN COLONIAL TIMES THAN NOW, IS AN APPEALING VARIATION ON HEAVIER FABRICS OFTEN ASSOCIATED WITH HOUSES OF THAT PERIOD. THIS PATTERN COMPLEMENTS THE LARGE COLLECTION OF PINK TRANSFERWARE. THE DOOR NEXT TO THE WINDOWS KEEPS THE TELEVISION OUT OF SIGHT.

Most of the furniture is antique, with a few newer upholstered pieces based on traditional styles. Ann and Mark love to come upon a good find, and travel provides opportunities to search in areas where Colonial-era pieces still may be available. Years ago, on a buying trip to England, they found the dining room hutch (called an oak dresser there) and their Georgian dining room table. They also purchased the large painted settle that anchors their entry hall. Originally used for seating, the piece features deep wings that protected against drafts; now it's a handy spot to deposit keys and caps.

To an observer with 18th-century sensibilities, the accessories would be familiar. Each piece has been lovingly collected, and all are authentic. Ann has a knack for displaying those things her family actually uses or finds interesting, so shelves hold dishes and glassware, bookcases have reference books, and tables showcase her collections. She has a number of George and Martha Washington framed silhouettes, and Mark indulges his Revolutionary War fascination by collecting miniature redcoats and minutemen. (CONTINUED ON PAGE 150)

LEFT Toile fabric and transferware have something in common: both celebrate rural scenes of Colonial times. They are a happy match in the dining room, where host and hostess chairs enhance the dignity of a table set with 19th-century Staffordshire china and crystal. First made in the 1750s, antique transferware is highly prized by collectors.

PAGES 148 AND 149 Though not authentic, the well-fitted kitchen and breakfast room have many Colonial elements. Cabinets are made to look like freestanding cupboards; glass doors on the upper part display dishes and glassware. The old-brick fireplace has a wrought-iron crane of the type once used to hold kettles and cooking pots.

Mark and Ann have overcome the dark atmosphere often found in period homes. With the changes they have made, their home has the breezy informality that their family enjoys and the historical integrity they crave. It also gives the couple the chance to live with the things they love. "Every time we drive up," Ann says, "I think, 'It's just perfect.'"

ABOVE STORAGE UNDER THE EAVES MAKES USE OF ALL AVAILABLE SPACE. THE WINDOW SEAT ALSO LIFTS FOR STORAGE AND LOOKS OUT OVER A LAKE.

RIGHT THE MASTER BEDROOM FEATURES A BOTANICAL PRINT IN GENTLE PASTELS, USED AT THE WINDOWS, IN BED LINENS, AND ON THE SLIPPER CHAIR. DARK WOOD AND PAINTED FURNITURE LEND WEIGHT FOR VISUAL BALANCE.

PAGE 152 SOOTHING BLUISH-GREEN IS THE OWNERS' FAVORITE SHADE FOR GARDEN FURNITURE BECAUSE IT BLENDS WITH NATURE'S OWN COLORS.

PAGES 152–153 THE BRICK FLOOR IN THE LIGHT-FILLED SUNROOM ONLY LOOKS AS THOUGH IT'S OLD. WORKERS USED SALVAGED BRICK AND DELIBERATELY WIDE MORTAR JOINTS TO ACHIEVE ITS RUGGEDLY AGED APPEARANCE.

# 3 Collector's Influence

# Masters of the Hunt

TWO FREE SPIRITS LIVE THE LIFE OF COUNTRY GENTLEMEN, FILLING THEIR 1799 HOME WITH ANTIQUES AND HUNTING MEMORABILIA.

LEFT AMONG THE MANY ITEMS WITH A HUNTING THEME, THIS SET OF PAINTED GLASSWARE DEPICTS VARIOUS SCENES OF HUNTSMEN IN TRADITIONAL RED GARB.

OPPOSITE THE RESTORED BARN IS HOME TO THE HORSES FRED ROOT KEEPS FOR RIDING TO THE HOUNDS.

LEFT THE LIVING
ROOM HAD ALL-WHITE
MOLDINGS WHEN FRED
ROOT AND ANTHONY FEO
FOUND THEIR HOME. A
DECORATIVE PAINTER
ADDED A FAUX-WOOD
FINISH, THEN PAINTED A
NEW SURROUND FOR THE
FIREPLACE TO MATCH. THE
HOMEOWNERS PREFER
DEEP-TONED WALLS AS
THE BACKGROUND FOR
THEIR COLLECTIONS. THE
VENERABLE GEORGE III
LEATHER CHAIR WAS AN
AUCTION FIND.

It's morning, and the sun is breaking through hazy clouds over Houndstooth Farm in Bedminster, New Jersey. Down in the barn, horses whinny as they reach soft muzzles into their hay. Meanwhile, Fred Root and Anthony Feo eat breakfast and prepare for the hunt. Both men anticipate a busy day, but each is thinking of a different search.

For Fred, the hunt means saddling up and looking for a fox; for Anthony, it's a quest for some "new" antique. Their interests coincide in their home and at their antiques and accessories store, Houndstooth, where dogs and horses are the order of the day.

The late-18th-century farmhouse they bought in 2000 is a country gentleman's dream, surrounded by 1,800 acres of prime hunting land, used by the Essex Fox Hounds. It's only the latest in a long line of homes—29, to be exact—that the pair has bought to renovate over the years. This one has four bedrooms and two stories, giving them ample space to fill with antiques and objects in the tallyho style they favor.

"We collect a lot of stuff," Anthony says. "And," Fred chimes in, "we love mixing antiques with reproduction pieces." Only

a practiced eye can tell which is which, because they disdain anything not finely crafted, no matter its age.

While pursuing their individual hobbies, the two partners share a love of collecting. Staffordshire dogs, dog portraits, antique silver, Scottish tartans, hunting scenes, ornate walking sticks, or leather-bound books—if they see one of these items and like it, they'll probably buy it. Furniture, especially antiques from Great Britain and France, is another passion they share.

Fred and Anthony feel the same way about houses. Though not die-hard restorers, they have the fortitude and vision to bring a structure up to its full potential, even if it means undoing work done by a previous owner. "This house was

(CONTINUED ON PAGE 165)

ABOVE LEFT LIKE THE WALKING STICKS OF AN 18TH-CENTURY SQUIRE, THESE ANTIQUE CANES ARE KEPT READY FOR TREKS IN THE COUNTRY.

LEFT THE REALISTICALLY PAINTED PORCELAIN FOX AND HOUND ARE STIRRUP CUPS; HISTORICALLY SUCH ITEMS HELD LIBATIONS FOR THIRSTY HUNTERS.

OPPOSITE THE TALL-BACK ANTIQUE FRENCH CHAIR WITH BARLEY-TWIST LEGS IS ONE OF SIX THAT THE OWNERS HAVE COLLECTED OVER THE YEARS. THEY CHOSE A DEEP RED FABRIC WITH A BUMBLEBEE MOTIF—SYMBOL OF NAPOLEON IN THE EARLY 1800S—FOR THE UPHOLSTERY, ADDING BRASS NAILHEAD TRIM.

# Masters of the Hunt

**ABOVE** Although it's a reproduction, the dining room hutch is a fitting display case for the collection of antique silver. On the table, silver chargers, fine porcelain, and staghorn utensils promise hearty dining.

**RIGHT** A Hepplewhite table and English chairs have seen many dinner parties over the last 200 years or so. Menswear-plaid upholstery and linen toile at the windows complement the polished wood.

renovated about 25 years ago," Anthony explains. "Former owners did some modernizing—replacing some of the original windows, for example—so we felt our job was to remove many of the contemporary elements and bring back as much of the original house as we could."

The exterior of the house looks almost the same as it did when it was built in 1799. Fred and Anthony added a bluestone terrace and low-slung wall to complement the front door. Inside, golden heart pine floors and dark, aged beams instill a sense of history.

"When we bought the house, everything in the living room was painted white," Anthony says, "so we had a trompe l'oeil artist make all the plaster trim look like pine. The firebox

(CONTINUED ON PAGE 169)

OPPOSITE OPEN SHELVING STORES DISHES AND STAPLES CLOSE AT HAND. PAINTED CABINETS AND THE PLANK FLOOR ARE TRUE TO THE COLONIAL ORIGINS OF THE HOME.

ABOVE AN ANTIQUE DRAFTING TABLE PAIRED WITH NEW CHAIRS SERVES AS AN INFORMAL AREA FOR DINING.

**RIGHT** An enormous island, topped with granite, provides a showcase for Anthony's culinary talents. Friends often perch on the other side to engage in conversation while he works. Heavy ceiling beams allude to the home's rich history.

OPPOSITE IN THE
MASTER BEDROOM,
BUFF-TONE WALLS,
PLAID FLANNEL AT THE
WINDOWS, FAVORITE
BOOKS, AND AN ARMOIRE
DISGUISING THE
TELEVISION CREATE A
RESTFUL RETREAT.

RIGHT REFLECTED IN
THE FLOOR-TO-CEILING
WALNUT MIRROR, A
COLLECTION OF PRINTS
FROM A VINTAGE
MENSWEAR CATALOG
COVERS THE WALL IN THE
DRESSING ROOM.

was there, but we designed a mantel to build around it and had it faux-painted to match." They also painted the walls, using shades of hunter green, khaki, and gold. "We think dark colors show things off better," Fred says.

This may well be true, especially with their particular collections, and certainly the deep colors create a warm ambience for the casual entertaining the men often do. Burnished leather, natural linen, touchable velvets, and polished woods look substantial against the deep tones and stained wood. Windows are purposely free of fussy treatments; most have simple draperies that don't hinder the light. Fred says, "We didn't want to do anything to cover them up. The light coming in our south-facing front windows is pretty amazing."

Upstairs, light floods in through windows with plaid flannel draperies. In a concession to convenience, the master suite is divided into sleeping and dressing areas. The baths

**RIGHT** TWO VESSEL SINKS AND VINTAGE-LOOK FIXTURES CONTRIBUTE TO AN ILLUSION OF AGE IN THE MASTER BATH. WHITE TILE AND A BEADED-BOARD WAINSCOTING KEEP THE ROOM FROM LOOKING TOO DARK.

**BELOW** STAG-PATTERN WALLPAPER INSPIRED THE MATCHING SWAGGED WINDOW TREATMENT, MADE WITH NATURALLY SHED ANTLERS.

are newly remodeled but have vintage character that often comes only with age.

The kitchen and great-room, though, are the heart of their home, and it's there that the two spend the most time. Anthony is an inspired cook, and it's not unusual for him to whip up a picnic, jump in one of their two restored cars—probably the wood-paneled 1948 station wagon—and drive off with a couple of dogs to join Fred in the fields. Finding some shade under a gnarled tree, the men pull bone china and crystal stemware from an old wicker picnic case with leather straps. Then they pour some wine, raise their glasses, and drink to horse country and the hunt.

# Farmhouse Eclectic

A Missouri couple fell in love with this Greek Revival house, even before they owned it. Twenty years later, it's still a labor of love.

LEFT A SLENDER RAILING CURVES ITS WAY TO THE TOP OF A WINDING STAIR. BUILT SHORTLY AFTER THE CIVIL WAR ENDED, THE HOME HAS SUBSTANTIAL YET FAIRLY SIMPLE MOLDINGS.

OPPOSITE PAIRED WITH BRANCH CORAL IN AN IRONSTONE TUREEN, THE ANTIQUE FRAME HOLDS FOUR MID-19TH-CENTURY CONCHOLOGY PRINTS.

# Farmhouse Eclectic

**LEFT** GENTLE DOVE
GRAY AND CREAM MAKE
A QUIET BACKGROUND
FOR THE ANTIQUE
FURNISHINGS IN
THE LIVING ROOM.
HOMEOWNER SUZEDIE
CLEMENTS COVERED
THE VINTAGE RADIATOR
WITH GRILLS FOR A
MORE FORMAL LOOK. IN
1987, SHE PAINTED AN
AMERICAN PRIMITIVE-
STYLE PORTRAIT OF HER
DAUGHTER, MARNY; IT
NOW HANGS ABOVE AN
EMPIRE PEDESTAL TABLE.

Those who share Suzedie Clements's love of antiques and older houses understand perfectly when she says, "I would want someone from the 1860s to be comfortable here." It's not that she's expecting 140-year-old guests; it's that she would like to be so sensitive to the spirit of her 1868 home that she'd only decorate it in a way that's appropriate.

She and her husband, Buck, first saw their farmhouse near St. Louis, Missouri, in the early 1970s when it was on a house tour. Instantly, they were smitten. The house wore its age with dignity, like so many homes of its era. With a simple Greek Revival style and full-width front porch, it also reminded Suzedie of time spent at her beloved grandparents' home in Tennessee. "The floor plans are identical," she says. "This place just felt like home."

When the house came on the market in 1986, the couple snapped it up—and they've been working on it ever since. It's been more than 20 years, so far, but no one is eager to call it finished, because the process is so much fun.

Ever since she can remember, Suzedie has been interested in antiques. As a small child, she tagged along with her

(CONTINUED ON PAGE 179)

**ABOVE** ANTIQUE NEWEL POSTS OFTEN HAVE A MOTHER-OF-PEARL PIECE SET INTO THE TOP—A TRADITION TO SHOW THAT THE ORIGINAL MORTGAGE WAS FINALLY PAID.

**RIGHT** TRANSFERWARE AND STAFFORDSHIRE DOGS ARE ENGLISH COUNTRY ANTIQUES. THE WOOD-MOSAIC TUNBRIDGEWARE BOX WAS MADE TO HOLD TEA.

LEFT Documentary wallpaper in the music room is a historical pattern from the 1857 home of prominent New Orleans architect James Gallier, Jr. The eclectic room combines an Eastlake walnut table and a portrait of Suzedie's father as a boy, painted by her aunt.

RIGHT Bright green hedge apples, which are also called Osage oranges, are not edible. Their nubby textures and rounded shapes lend themselves to a lovely display.

parents as they rooted through antiques stores. She helped drag their treasures home and watched as they decorated. Her aunt, Edith Brazwell Evans, was editor of a design magazine in the 1950s. Suzedie was constantly exposed to the good, the bad, and the dusty, and she learned at an early age to distinguish the differences. Now she puts that knowledge to good use in her own vintage home.

"It's my dream house," she says, referring to the way her 10-room home looks now. She had to work, though, to make it happen. Although she and Buck appreciated the graceful structure from the first time they saw it, the bland interiors did nothing to stir her feelings.

Suzedie, a trained artist with a playful side, has a love of color, texture, art, and nature. Bringing home a shell or whorl of wood to admire its design comes as naturally to her as breathing. Besides having an ample supply of family heirlooms, Suzedie is prone to collect many different things—antique pottery, Empire Period furniture, 19th-century prints, whatever. Anywhere she lives must be eclectic enough to tolerate what she likes at the moment or decides to collect. And after all these years, her old home doesn't blink an eye.

"I didn't have a plan," Suzedie says. "I just wanted each room to be 'true'." She "plays around" until each room seems right, using pastels and jewel tones, decorative painting and wallpaper, florals and plaids, mahogany and painted pieces, antiques and reproductions. Such a broad range might well produce chaotic results, but instead, the couple's home has an inviting ambience. This is because underneath it all, there are two constants: Suzedie's tastes and her desire to reflect the inherent character of the house.

Greek Revival-style homes were most popular from about 1820 to 1850. Homes sprang up in Boston and Philadelphia, and the style, based on classic Greek architecture, gradually worked its way out to the rougher frontier. After the Civil War, Missouri became more settled as former soldiers headed west to start new lives. By the time the Clementses' home

ABOVE MAJOLICA POTTERY WORKS WELL WITH BROWN TRANSFERWARE, SAYS SUZEDIE. THE LATE- 1800S CAULIFLOWER TEAPOT IS A RARE PIECE, MADE BY GRIFFEN, SMITH & HILL OF PENNSYLVANIA.

OPPOSITE RIPE-TOMATO WALLS IN THE DINING ROOM SET OFF POLISHED MAHOGANY AND GREEN MAJOLICA. THE CHIPPENDALE-STYLE CHAIRS WERE A GIFT FROM BUCK'S PARENTS.

OPPOSITE
Transferware
designs are taken
from etchings and
transferred on paper
to the surface of the
pottery. Transferware
was developed in
18th-century England,
reaching its height in
the 19th century.

RIGHT This antique
transferware,
collected wherever
the Clementses can
find it, is on display
until it's needed. Most
of their collection is
in regular use.

was built, Greek Revival was freer; away from big cities, experienced architects, materials, and knowledgeable craftspeople weren't always available. Proportions relaxed, moldings became simpler, and local materials supplanted imported plaster medallions.

The vernacular architecture is far more accepting of eclectic interiors than its Eastern cousins would be. "I like layering different styles, because a family would have had furniture passed down through the generations," Suzedie says. She lets each room determine its own style. In the dining room, music room, and living room, she leans a little toward formal furnishings, with documentary wallpaper, marble fireplaces, and inlaid mahogany, Empire, or Eastlake walnut furniture. Color runs the gamut from soft dove gray to vibrant tomato red, which is one of her favorite shades. "Furniture looks great against red," says Suzedie,

LEFT Developing her own technique for reverse-stenciled fernwork—a Victorian craft—Suzedie decorated a demilune wicker table. Years ago, her aunt pressed the delicate ferns now displayed in a frame.

OPPOSITE Piled high with hand-stitched cotton quilts, the 1830s-era carved tester bed is a favorite spot to catch a nap.

who especially likes red with deep mahogany. As a fine-arts major, she knows her colors, accenting the red with its complement, green, in antique majolica on the sideboard.

Empire furniture, too, is a favorite, and Suzedie probably has more of it than any other style. In the hallway, it goes formal in mahogany or has a countrified feeling in tiger maple, acting as a bridge between areas with various degrees of formality.

In more private rooms, comfort and livability are Suzedie's only goals, yet she uses period pieces to achieve them. A carved tester bed, made in 1830 and layered with linens, is the highlight of the master bedroom—so comfortable that people and pets alike appreciate it.

The kitchen, though renovated, has antique trappings to make it cozy. Brown transferware, collected over many

years, is displayed on newly painted putty green walls as art until Suzedie needs to use it. Patina and a few odd nicks don't bother Suzedie a bit. "I love furniture that is well-used," she says. "Condition means nothing to me if the piece is beautiful." Spoken like an artist. Or an antiques lover. Or someone who enjoys her things.

Several years ago, at the urging of clients, Suzedie started an interior design business with her friend Laura Miller. "Framing art was the start of our business," she explains. "Clients wanted accessories to go with the artwork, and soon we were decorating whole houses." Most of those residences aren't as old as Suzedie's, but each of them does have a unique character. Designing to achieve a specific look isn't a problem, because the two concentrate on capturing the character and spirit of that particular place—and it usually works. When the spirit is right, the home is right, and whoever might come will feel comfortable.

OPPOSITE LAZY DAYS ON THE PORCH ARE MORE COMFORTABLE BECAUSE IT IS FURNISHED WITH WICKER FROM THE 1920S.

ABOVE BUILT IN 1868, THE VERNACULAR GREEK REVIVAL FARMHOUSE HAS SQUARED DORIC COLUMNS, A FULL-WIDTH PORCH, AND A SHALLOW ROOFLINE. BY THE TIME THIS STYLE REACHED THE MISSOURI "FRONTIER," IT WAS MUCH LESS FORMAL THAN "BACK EAST."

# Precious Legacy

Moving from a larger home to a condominium near the city, this Boston couple brought along memories in their beloved family heirlooms.

LEFT Fresh flowers complement the pastel living room, where antiques, heirlooms, and a few newer furnishings form a harmonious balance.

OPPOSITE The Napoleonic-style daybed is a treasured piece. Gilded French sconces and a graceful carved table add formality.

OPPOSITE QUEEN ANNE-STYLE FURNITURE WITH CURVING CABRIOLE LEGS ADDS A DELICATE NOTE AMONG MORE SUBSTANTIAL UPHOLSTERED PIECES.

RIGHT THE OVERSIZE CAST-STONE FIREPLACE, FOCAL POINT OF THE LIVING ROOM, FEATURES A NATURALISTIC OAK-LEAF MOTIF. CHINESE LACQUERWARE ADDS ITS DISTINCTIVE RED COLOR TO THE MANTEL.

The maxim that "children learn what they live with" seems especially true in the realm of decorating and furnishing a home. Interior designer Jane Forman, a Bostonian with a master's touch in combining fabrics and furnishings, credits her mother and grandmother with any success she has had.

"I grew up steeped in design," she says, referring to her mother's career as an antiques dealer and her grandmother's good eye for furniture. "My mother did a lot of her own decorating and kept refining her style through the years. My grandmother's things were classic and had quality, so they were worth keeping."

The family talent is still alive, as evidenced in the new condominium that Jane and her husband, Charles, occupy. When they sold their larger Tudor home in the suburbs and moved to Brookline, Massachusetts, just west of Boston, they might have considered shedding their old furnishings and starting fresh. They're not that kind of people, though.

To the Formans, furniture is about more than having a place to sit. It's the repository of family memories and lifelong learning; they've inherited that crucial attitude along with the chairs and love seats. "I'm lucky they had good taste," Jane says of her relatives.

Starting with this firm foundation, the couple has developed its own style. Over the years, Jane has taken to heart the knowledge she learned as she grew up and has become a master at choosing color and fabrics to keep older pieces looking up-to-date.

The living room, for instance, is a study in taupe and pale blue, with Queen Anne-style and French furniture fitted out in lush fabrics—cut velvet, quilted cotton, and a hybrid leopard-and floral-medallion print. This comfortable space has relatively few accessories, but each one holds its own because of its quality.

A cast-iron daybed at one end of the room has a bank of pillows in a mix of fabrics. Gilded sconces flank a bas-relief carving, and the French coffee table, embellished with pierced foliate carving, lends a sense of old Europe. (CONTINUED ON PAGE 197)

ABOVE A DISPLAY OF ANTIQUE TORTOISESHELL, GROUPED FOR EMPHASIS ON THE 1920S SECRETARY, ADDS WARMTH IN TONES OF GOLD AND BROWN.

OPPOSITE CHINESE PORCELAIN, ASSEMBLED OVER THE YEARS, AND TORTOISESHELL BOXES BOTH SHOW UP HANDSOMELY AGAINST THE LIGHT-COLOR PAINTED FURNITURE.

OPPOSITE Canton ware commonly features images of a pagoda, a bridge, trees, and often a boat. A scalloped inner border distinguishes Canton ware from similar pottery called Nanking ware. From the late 17th to the 19th century, Chinese-export pieces came to Europe and later America in the holds of sailing ships—hence their lesser-known name, ballast ware.

LEFT Custom-made bookcases with arched openings provide elegant shelving for books and for the Canton ware, named for Canton, the Chinese city where this type of blue-and-white porcelain was made.

195

OPPOSITE A NEW, RED TOLE CHANDELIER IS AN INFORMAL ACCENT IN THE DINING ROOM, WHICH FEATURES FRENCH FABRICS AND FURNITURE HANDED DOWN WITHIN THE FAMILY.

RIGHT Classic French FURNITURE AND A COLOR SCHEME OF YELLOW AND BLUE—À LA PROVENCE— MAKE AN IDEAL SETTING FOR A COLLECTION OF QUIMPER POTTERY FOUND ON THE FORMANS' TRAVELS IN EUROPE.

Jane especially treasures the blue and white Canton porcelain she uses in almost every room. The Formans received a few pieces from Jane's family when they first married, and as they have traveled over the years, they've amassed quite a large amount. "I'm so attracted to the blue and white," Jane says. "It can blend with almost any decor. And the shapes are beautiful; it's classic and timeless." She adds, "My parents collected it for many, many years. Growing up with their collection has inspired my own interest and has made for a wonderful family connection."

Jane and Charles also like the colorful painted designs of French Quimper pottery, on display in the dining room; the collection is surrounded by family furniture with the same informal attitude. Vibrant yellow, blue, and red fabric and accessories capture an authentic country-French feel. With tumbled Jerusalem limestone flooring and a blend of natural wood and painted furniture, the room achieves just the right balance.

The Formans bought their condominium before it was complete, so Jane was able to make crucial decisions that helped her decorate it to suit her tastes. The contractors reconfigured

LEFT A MICROCOSM OF COUNTRY-FRENCH STYLE, ONE CORNER FEATURES FLOWERS IN A QUIMPER WARE PITCHER, SCENIC TOILE PAPER ON A PROVINCIAL TABLE, AND STYLIZED FLORAL FABRIC AT THE WINDOW.

OPPOSITE A SKILLFUL MIX OF PATTERNED AND CHECK FABRICS IS A HALLMARK OF TRADITIONAL STYLE.

PAGES 200–201 IN THE MASTER BEDROOM GENTLE COLORS AND TOUCHABLE FABRICS IN DELICATE BOTANICAL MOTIFS CREATE SOFTNESS. THE PLUMP LOVE SEAT IS AN OLD FAMILY PIECE.

the rooms, and Jane chose any material she wanted as a surface. "There were no restrictions," Jane says. "I was able to customize every building material; that was part of the appeal." Moldings are wide, and fixtures are traditional, in keeping with the history-minded style of the home. She opted for a custom-made cast-stone fireplace in the living room and later arranged the room around it.

Because their old bedroom furniture was not well-suited for their new home, the Formans left it behind. Jane chose a French-inspired four-poster bed with an upholstered headboard and footboard. It teams up with the love seat Jane's grandmother once owned, so now the master bedroom is a sitting room too. As in the rest of their home, color and

(CONTINUED ON PAGE 203)

OPPOSITE THE FRENCH
DAYBED IN PEWTER-
FINISH STEEL SERVES AS
A SOFA IN THE OFFICE AND
DOUBLES AS AN EXTRA
BED FOR GUESTS. THE
LARGE-SCALE TOILE DE
JOUY PATTERN ON WALLS
AND SEATING IS DILUTED
WITH OFF-WHITE IN
FURNITURE AND FABRICS.

LEFT AN HEIRLOOM
BREAKFAST ROOM CHAIR,
NEWLY COVERED IN A
HUNTING-SCENE TOILE,
SERVES AS A DESK CHAIR
IN THE OFFICE.

fabrics play a major role in creating the ambience. The primary fabric is a smooth-to-the-touch floral in pastels against an off-white ground; it is a pretty interpretation of a classic design. Other pattern is minimal: a striated wallpaper, subtly striped carpet, and embroidered borders on the bed linens.

Jane's office is another story entirely. She revels in the large-scale crimson and cream wallpaper that is its dominant element; she even uses the pattern for upholstery on her daybed and office chair, a Queen Anne-style legacy from her mother's breakfast room. Like many home offices, this one sometimes serves as a guest room, and the daybed becomes a place to sleep.

"In my old house," Jane says, "I used more intense colors and pattern that looked right in its Tudor setting. In this new and very different home, I've opted for more neutral coloring in the living room and master bedroom, with bold colors in the family room and my home office." There's another difference too: Owning a condo means maintenance-free living, with no lawn requiring care and nothing to keep the Formans from traveling. It still feels like home when they return, though, because family history and memories are present in every room.

# Genteel Jewel

TUCKED IN A NEIGHBORHOOD OF MUCH GRANDER HOMES, THIS TINY TREASURE LIVES AS ELEGANTLY AS ANY OF THEM.

LEFT A HUDSON RIVER-STYLE MURAL PAINTED BY A LOCAL ARTIST GIVES DRAMATIC CHARACTER TO THE WALLS OF THE POWDER ROOM.

OPPOSITE AN ANTIQUE DROP-FRONT SECRETARY FILLED WITH BOOKS STANDS WITH ITS DOORS PERMANENTLY OPEN. AS A RESULT, PAINTINGS HANG LOWER THAN USUAL IN AN EYE-CATCHING DISPLAY.

S

Sheila Barron laughs as she describes the difference between her home and other Georgian and Colonial homes on her street in Evanston, Illinois. "Mine is just a 'mansion-in-miniature,'" she says. Indeed, at 2,000 square feet, it is much smaller than most of her neighbors' three-story homes, but the converted carriage house makes up for its comparatively small size with well-bred attitude and well-appointed style.

Set far from the street on a property with 200 feet of formal gardens in front, the formerly nondescript house is the fulfillment of a dream. "After living in apartments all my life, I wanted a turn at living in a home with property," says Sheila. "When I saw this house, I was taken with the romance of it." Although the front gardens were much larger than she had envisioned, the small area behind the house was fine because, as Sheila says, "All I really wanted in the back was a little screened porch or terrace where I could read and have a glass of lemonade."

Sheila and her daughter, Laura Stoll, are both well-known interior designers. They immediately saw the potential for a marvelous home, though "marvelous" was a long way off.

LEFT Vibrant shades of the sunset in a favorite painting above the fireplace inspired a warm color palette, set off by white.

ABOVE Tilted forward, the oversize French mirror reflects the entire room, making it seem larger. Pumpkin-color walls, a bare floor, and a contemporary glass table loosen up the traditional style.

Previous remodeling had modernized the interior, but it had also destroyed any semblance of character linking the structure to its Georgian origins. Inside, the house looked like a 1950s-era cottage.

The two women knew that if they were to bring it back with architectural integrity, they would have to add details such as moldings and French doors. "At first, I thought I could just raise the ceilings here and add a little molding there, and it would be a snap. But it turned out it was more cost-effective to gut the house and start over than it was to patch up bad work," Sheila says. And so a labor of love began.

The immediate need was to open up the downstairs and raise the unbearably low ceilings, which were only 7 feet high in places. The two did away with a closet, increasing the size of the living room to 17×17 feet, and rerouted plumbing pipes to the upstairs bathrooms, which allowed them to raise the ceiling.

ABOVE AT A MERE 8 FEET SQUARE, THE KITCHEN IS UNDENIABLY SMALL. SHEILA OPTED TO USE ONLY BASE CABINETS, DESIGNING THEM TO LOOK LIKE FURNITURE.

RIGHT LEATHER-BOUND BOOKS ADD WARMTH AND CHARACTER TO A CORNER OF THE LIVING ROOM WHERE A SELDOM-USED DOOR ONCE WAS. HANGING PAINTINGS FROM THE BOOKCASE MAXIMIZES THE SPACE.

LEFT Extending into former attic space, a tray ceiling adds drama to the sitting room, which the owner also uses as a workroom. The antique Flemish screen is her favorite possession.

RIGHT In the powder room, a breathtaking mural covers the walls. A gilded Italian console was fitted with a marble top and plumbing fixtures to create a vanity.

The kitchen is still small—a mere 8×8 feet—yet it is highly functional and makes an attractive serving area for the dining room. Sheila accomplished this by opting not to have upper cabinets, designing lower cabinets to look like furniture, and placing the refrigerator out of sight in the adjoining pantry.

Upstairs, a portion of the attic is now raised, allowing for an impressive 12-foot tray ceiling over the sitting room/workroom at the top of the stairs, where Sheila often sees clients. Three upstairs bedrooms became two bedroom/bath suites—one for Sheila and one for her own mother, who until recently lived with her—and each has ample storage.

All this construction had to take place before Sheila and Laura could tackle the most enjoyable part of the project—decorating to bring character back to the rooms. "One of the highlights of the house is the millwork. We spared no expense with that," Sheila says. "We have three-piece, 9-inch moldings and extra-wide door casings throughout the house, including the bathrooms and bedrooms. We also put in a magnificent railing to the upstairs."

Although a traditional aesthetic guided many of their decisions, tradition occasionally leaned toward a more contemporary outlook to keep the home on its toes: In the living room, bare floors and a large glass-top coffee table and two chairs with a pieced upholstery treatment are unexpectedly fresh. The dining room also serves as a library, and the kitchen, with its gleaming hand-rubbed cabinetry, looks like one big buffet.

Color, however, presented the most exciting challenge. In the public rooms, warm color comes from a 19th-century landscape painting from the Hudson River school. Hanging in

the living room, the piece commands attention and is so arresting that Sheila and Laura decided the walls should follow its lead. "We tried all sorts of yellows and golds, but this acorn squash or pumpkin is the color we kept coming back to. It's just yummy," Sheila says. The pumpkin shade sets off her mainly dark-wood and white-upholstered furniture beautifully. Gilded frames, lush fabrics, period landscape paintings, a magnificent collection of leather-bound books, and glittering crystal light fixtures add richness and texture. "I've always had an off-white scheme and nothing else," says Sheila. "It took a lot of courage for us to go ahead and do this, but I know I won't get tired of it. I feel warm and fuzzy in this house."

RIGHT WARM PUMPKIN REVERTS TO AN ACCENT COLOR IN THIS BEDROOM BUILT AROUND BOTANICAL PRINTS IN SHADES OF GREEN.

PAGE 214 ENORMOUS CARVED FRENCH CORBELS FORM A DRAMATIC BASE FOR THE VANITY IN THE MASTER BATH. ANTIQUE LANDSCAPE PAINTINGS HELP UNIFY THE ROOMS.

PAGE 215 BY KEEPING TO ONE—AND ONLY ONE—DESIGN MOTIF FOR HER BEDROOM, SHEILA IS FREE TO LAVISH IT ON WALLS AND FABRIC WITHOUT THE ROOM BECOMING TOO BUSY. WHITE WOODWORK AND THE LIGHT BACKGROUND OF THE DESIGN KEEP THE SMALL ROOM FROM CLOSING IN. TEXTURE AND DARK-WOOD FURNITURE ADD VISUAL WEIGHT.

# British
# Accent

## This California 'manor' looks as authentic as any from across the pond.

LEFT QUARRIED STONE WALLS, GRACEFUL WOODWORK, AND LUSH GREEN SURROUNDINGS GIVE THE DISTINCT IMPRESSION THAT THIS IS A HOME IN THE ENGLISH COUNTRYSIDE.

OPPOSITE AN EASY MIX OF FRENCH, ENGLISH, ITALIAN, AND HEIRLOOM FURNITURE SUITS THE CHARACTER OF THIS SAN DIEGO HOME, WHERE THE EDWARDS FAMILY LIVES AND RAISES HORSES. THE STAIRWAY RUNNER COMBINES COLORS USED THROUGHOUT THE DOWNSTAIRS ROOMS.

LEFT Impressively traditional in its architecture, the home is alive with yellows and golds. Interior designer Hank Morgan added brighter colors and crisp white trim to transform the formerly dreary house to one that is much more livable. Dark-stained flooring and textured surfaces help keep the vibrant color in check.

Visitors to this home near San Diego can't believe their eyes: It looks just like an authentic British manor house. From the weathered stone walls and shake roof to rose gardens just outside its doors, the house looks as if it were transplanted, completely intact, from jolly old England.

Linda and Marc Edwards purchased the home, built in the 1980s, a few years ago and were struck by its architectural integrity. "The house was gorgeous," Linda says, "and I absolutely love English architecture." Even more impressive was its site—5½ acres of rolling pastureland—which was ideal for the family's horses. "Honestly, what impressed me the most was the barn. That was the real reason for moving here," she adds.

The family spent the next 10 years developing the property into a small ranch where they could indulge their passion for horses, even building a small riding arena and trails. They worked their way up to the house, creating gardens, making major improvements to the pool area, and adding a cabana. Finally, two years ago, with their four children in college, Marc and Linda decided to revamp the inside of their home.

When redoing previous homes, Linda had turned to a childhood friend, Hank Morgan, now a leading interior designer in Southern California. "I've known Hank my whole life," she says. "We grew up together in Newport Beach. He never makes mistakes." It was time to call on his services again.

Morgan was duly impressed by what he terms "the good bones and magnificent architectural detail" of the house. Still, he adds, "Over the years it had become dreary and rather lifeless." He decided to reinforce its inherently English country-home character then rev it up a notch with color.

Linda and Marc had quite a few family pieces and other antiques that Morgan wanted to incorporate. To make them stand out, he created more contrast. For walls in the public areas, he chose a sunny yellow, a fresh choice only a few steps away from the mineral-based ocher yellow used in 18th-century homes. He freshened the woodwork by painting the wainscoting, pilasters, crown molding, arched doorways, and window and door trim with clean crisp white, covering up the previous bland vanilla. "Before, the architectural details were barely noticeable," Linda says. "The white paint really made them pop."

With dreary color no longer an issue, Morgan was free to give the floors a dark stain, setting up an interplay of brights and darks. Against the foundation of mellow oak floors, needlepoint and textured sisal rugs also assume more importance. (CONTINUED ON PAGE 225)

ABOVE SURROUNDED BY 5½ ACRES OF ROLLING GROUNDS, THE EDWARDS HOME HAS A WEATHERED STONE EXTERIOR, A SHAKE ROOF, AND DIVIDED-LIGHT WINDOWS WITH GRACEFUL ELLIPTICAL TRANSOMS.

OPPOSITE THREE STEPS UP FROM THE LIVING ROOM, A GALLERY OFFERS SEATING WITH A VIEW OF THE LANDSCAPED TERRACE. FLORAL DRAPERIES ADD ANOTHER "OUTDOOR" ELEMENT.

LEFT One of the first purchases Linda and Marc Edwards made for their new home was the painting of a gold-bedecked horse that now hangs in the living room. Its large scale and rich colors make other artwork at that end of the room unnecessary. Dark accents, wood, and a deep-green sofa echo the background colors of the painting, adding more depth. The antique wood carving of Quan Yin, the Buddhist deity of compassionate loving kindness, is one of several Asian pieces.

223

OPPOSITE THE 42x24-FOOT LIVING ROOM HAS SEVERAL CONVERSATION GROUPINGS THAT MAKE IT MORE INTIMATE FOR SMALLER GATHERINGS. TIERED WALLS AND A CARVED-MARBLE MANTEL ARE DRAMATIC COMPLEMENTS TO THE FURNISHINGS. PAINTED DETAILING ON THE CROWN MOLDING HIGHLIGHTS INDIVIDUAL DENTILS.

RIGHT A FLORAL STRIPE IS A UNIFYING ELEMENT IN THIS ROOM, COVERING THE ARMCHAIR AT ONE END OF THE ROOM AND A PAIR OF SOFAS AT THE OTHER. SOLIDS, STRIPES, AND TRIMMINGS PROVIDE VARIETY AND VISUAL INTEREST.

Much of the furniture—traditional French, English, Italian, and American antiques, reproductions, and family heirlooms—is also polished wood, delighting the eye with more subtle contrasts.

"The combination of pieces gives a kind of collected look to the furnishings," Morgan says. "The rooms don't look as if they were just invented, but as if they evolved over generations. That gives a relatively new English-style house an authentic English character."

Linda might well have balked if Morgan had insisted on replacing her cherished antiques. "A lot of the furniture we have came from my mother and has been in our family 50 or 60 years. To me [these pieces] are as familiar as old family friends, and I love having them around," she says.

Morgan reupholstered antique chairs and sofas in more youthful fabrics, choosing a yellow floral as the predominant pattern downstairs. In the living room and adjacent stone-walled gallery, the flowered yellow stripe creates unity among rooms and brings in a refreshing touch of the outdoors.

Because it is so large, the living room might have presented a problem; the solution was to create islands in the sea of space. Morgan designed several seating areas that effectively divide the room, anchoring each with an area rug and giving each a focal point. At one end, two floral sofas flank a fireplace topped by an antique portrait of a child at play. At the other,

a painting of a magnificent prancing horse reigns above another grouping. This end has a mossy-green sofa, but pillows and an upholstered chair share the floral fabric, so the room looks pulled together. The arrangement is suitable for a crowd of guests, yet allows more intimate conversation in small groups too.

The dining room is more formal in tone, although it shares the same color palette. For this room, Morgan chose a Chinese wallpaper, meticulously hand-painted in the same colors used for the living room. With polished antique furniture, gilded mirrors, a crystal chandelier, and silver serving pieces, the refurbished room has a decidedly Georgian ambience.

The kitchen was outdated and needed more than a mere facelift. The owners tore out several small rooms, combining them into one space with convivial sitting and dining areas that would make an English pub-goer feel at home.

(CONTINUED ON PAGE 231)

RIGHT Hand-painted Chinese wallpaper—a classic design of flowering plants with exotic birds—harmonizes with fabric on the French-style chairs in the dining room. A silver-and-crystal epergne complements the formal dinnerware. On the sideboard, the tea service and inlaid liquor cabinet are British antiques.

LEFT COMBINING SMALLER ROOMS CREATED ONE LARGE ROOM FOR AN ENGLISH COUNTRY KITCHEN WITH ELEMENTS OF A COZY TAVERN. WALNUT CABINETS HAVE SMOOTH GRANITE COUNTERTOPS AND PRESSED-TIN BACKSPLASHES. A MASSIVE PEWTER EXHAUST HOOD HANGS ABOVE THE MARBLE-TOPPED COOKING ISLAND. AN OLD-BRICK FLOOR, VARIOUS WINE IMPLEMENTS, AND AN EXTENSIVE COLLECTION OF PEWTER SERVING PIECES FURTHER THE ILLUSION OF A PUB.

OPPOSITE ACROSS FROM THE SINK, A WOK STATION SUPPLEMENTS THE ISLAND COOKTOP. A WINE RACK KEEPS BOTTLES AT THE READY.

RIGHT BROAD WINDOWS IN THE SITTING ROOM LOOK OUT TO THE HORSE PASTURE. BRICK FLOORING CONTINUES FROM THE ADJOINING KITCHEN BUT HERE, IT'S DIVIDED INTO SQUARES BY WOODEN PLANKS.

BELOW RIGHT CABINETS DESIGNED FOR DISPLAY AND EASY ACCESS EVOKE THE FEELING OF A PUB.

Simple wood cabinets have authentically shaped detailing, hand-rubbed with a golden-brown finish that looks as old as the worn-brick floor. Stone countertops, a pressed-tin backsplash, and tattersall wallpaper add to the effect. The crowning touch, however, is a sculptural pewter hood above the center island. Nearby shelves display the couple's collection of softly gleaming pewter serving pieces.

"This is a very large house," Linda says, "and all of it gets used, but the kitchen area is where we really and truly live. Our living spaces don't stop at the walls, though. They extend to the patios and even the pastures and, come to think of it, all the way to the barn."

# 4 Lighthearted Spirit

# The Royal Smile

THIS HOME, THOUGH
SMALL, HAS A KINGDOM OF
GOOD IDEAS, MIXING ART AND
OBJECTS IN A HUMOROUS
YET STYLISH BLEND.

LEFT THE PILLOWS ARE
MADE FROM VINTAGE
ITALIAN UNIFORMS IN
BLACK WOOL WITH
GOLDEN BRAID.

OPPOSITE NEOCLASSIC
ACCENTS COEXIST WITH
MORE RECENT PIECES.
A MODEL OF A PALLADIAN
DOME AND A MARQUETRY
CHEST FORM PART OF
AN ASYMMETRICAL
ARRANGEMENT ON AN
EARLY COLFAX & FOWLER
LACQUERED CABINET.

LEFT COLORS REPEAT FOR COHESIVENESS IN THE TINY SPACE: A REGENCY-ERA PAINTING OF CASTLES INTRODUCES A BIT OF RED, TYING IN WITH RED DINING ROOM CHAIR CUSHIONS (SEE PAGE 239). THE PILLOWS, LAMP SHADE, AND PICTURE FRAME SHARE DRAMATIC BLACK AND GOLD ACCENTS.

RIGHT AN OVERSIZE CLOCK FROM A FRENCH RAILROAD STATION TAKES THE PLACE OF MORE TRADITIONAL ARTWORK OVER THE STAIRWAY.

Heraldry runs rampant in the apartment of antiques dealer Lee Stanton. The tiny pied-à-terre makes up for its lack of size with an attitude that is positively kingly. Using his expertise at finding the perfect piece, Lee has furnished the space with items evoking images of royalty: an 18th-century Scottish terra-cotta lion (the king of beasts that Lee regards as his personal symbol), a Regency-Era castle painting, and an antique chessboard with kings and queens set to trounce the pawns. Crests and Gothic motifs crop up in every room, and with almost as much pomp as the royal original, a portrait of England's King George III on horseback surveys the living room.

Lee's home wasn't always his castle, however. When he decided to expand on his thriving gallery in San Juan Capistrano, an hour away, by setting up an antiques showroom in Los Angeles, he hoped to find a location with a place nearby where he could live. He searched for three years before coming upon this property, which he bought on the spot. The site includes a 1930s-era commercial building for the showroom as well as a two-story apartment building connected to it by a private courtyard, all in the bustling La Cienega/Melrose

design district. "I can live in the upstairs apartment, rent out the downstairs, and walk across the courtyard to the shop every day. Then on weekends, I drive back to my home in Laguna Beach," Lee says.

The property was in extremely derelict condition when he bought it, but Lee used its shortcomings as a springboard for stylish changes. "Stray cats had been living here several years, and the hardwood floors were ruined," he says. "But I knew I wanted a black-lacquered floor." He made a decision not to replace the damaged flooring and instead lacquered it to seal the wood and conceal its flaws. In the process, he set the stage for dramatic furnishings.

Changing the walls or adding doors to create more defined spaces was out of the question. "The walls are structural, so nothing could be taken out, and there's not enough room to open any doors," Lee explains. He decided to create a see-through screen between the living room and dining room by hanging antique wooden windows, hinged along one side.

Lee uses color as his chief tool to unify spaces and his furnishings, drawn from eras spanning a couple of centuries.

The background palette of black flooring, taupe walls, and neutral upholstery directs the eye toward accents of regal red and shimmering metallics, mainly gold. Using the same colors throughout the entire space makes it seem larger.

In the dining room, where simple chairs with bright red cushions vie with more pedigreed pieces for attention, Lee introduces the surprise element of turquoise glass on a 20th-century pedestal table. "The color holds this place together," Lee says. Whether inspired by royalty or not, furnishings from different periods are harmonious because of shared colors and, just as often, their shared themes.

The castle painting is a case in point. When Lee was pondering whether the red dining chair cushions would seem out of place with the more restrained living room, he remembered having this artwork. "It features red rooftops," he says. "I realized it was the pivotal piece I needed to make the chairs work." In fact, regal-red accents in the book spines, a pillow, and the painting of King George decree that "this thread of color shall unite these spaces into one harmonious whole."

OPPOSITE UNDER THE GAZE OF KING GEORGE III AND HIS HORSE, LEATHER-BOUND BOOKS LEND A SCHOLARLY TONE TO THE LIVING ROOM. FABRIC FOR THE PETIT-POINT PILLOW WAS SALVAGED FROM A RUINED TAPESTRY.

ABOVE RICHLY VEINED SPHERES OF ITALIAN MARBLE ARE DISPLAYED ON PEDESTALS. THESE CLASSICALLY INSPIRED DECORATING ELEMENTS, FAVORITES IN EUROPE, ADD VISUAL WEIGHT BELOW THE MIRROR.

ABOVE Cast in bronze, Minerva, Roman goddess of wisdom, rests on a pedestal by the door.

RIGHT Too tall to be handrests, posts on this late-19th-century English chair were originally designed to hold candles. Other lofty accents include architectural models on a hefty Scottish bedroom cupboard.

# Building Character

## High expectations convert a nondescript house into a tasteful vacation home.

OPPOSITE Elegant in its simplicity, the weathered-iron antique English bed is the crowning touch in the master bedroom.

LEFT The entryway sets a casual mood in the house with its diamond-pane doors and stairway railing, elements reminiscent of a traditional horse stable.

**LEFT** White upholstery acts as a foil for art and accessories in vibrant colors. Simple battens on plain walls take the place of more elaborate paneling.

**ABOVE** Built on the 30×30-foot foundation of a previous home, the Dutch-Colonial-style cottage now rises three stories, surrounded by such amenities as a pool and an acre of gardens.

For many years the house in a quiet seaside community in the Hamptons attracted no more than an occasional glance from neighbors who happened to be walking by. It was a short, stocky Cape Cod—a latecomer built on an infill lot surrounded by older, more impressive Victorian and Dutch Colonial homes. It wasn't especially bad; at the same time, it had little to recommend it.

Now it's a showstopper, a tall and lovely structure that commands attention as much for its beauty as for its transformation. Architect Stuart Disston, who had the vision to increase its height and change its character, says, "We modeled the style after the old shore houses that were built in the community."

His clients had formerly lived in England. After returning to the States, they began looking for an architecturally appealing beach house in a desirable location. They were disappointed to find that few houses had both attributes. They finally compromised and purchased the not-especially-attractive Cape Cod for its tree-filled acre lot with ample room for gardens. They loved the settled neighborhood too.

When Disston started his redesign, he realized that he would have to take the original house down to the ground if the home was to have the character his clients desired. "The old attic ceiling was only 7 feet high," he says. The 30×30 footprint was a satisfactory starting point for his plan.

"The original house was shaped in an L. We squared off the first floor with corner columns, then built the second floor up from there," Disston says. There are now two full stories, and the living space tucked into the new third-level attic has more than enough headroom.

The new plan revolves around a central stairwell, which is also key to setting the style of the house. Vertical wooden railings, painted crisp white and accented with a circular

ABOVE WALLS OF FLOOR-TO-CEILING BOOKCASES AND A PAINTED SETTEE STRETCHING SIDE TO SIDE MAXIMIZE THE ILLUSION OF SPACE IN THE NARROW LIBRARY BEHIND THE LIVING ROOM.

RIGHT THE HOUSE WRAPS AROUND A CENTRAL STAIRWELL. ALLUDING TO THE HOMEOWNER'S FAVORITE GAME, THE FIREPLACE FEATURES A GOLF-BALL-AND-CLUB THEME.

cutout, are replicas of those in New England's classic stables. Diamond-pane windows in the double-door entry work in tandem with the stairwell, offering a wordless introduction to the home's casual style.

On one side of the stairwell, the living room is a happy blend of white walls, pickled oak flooring, and vibrant accents. The fireplace surrenders some of its focal point status to the colorful contemporary art and bright pillows. White upholstery and a black-lacquered table create a neutral background that lets the artwork shine. Observant visitors, though, discover the humorous secret of the fireplace surround: Its carvings depict golf implements, a reference to the homeowner's fondness for the game. (CONTINUED ON PAGE 254)

LEFT THICK MARBLE COUNTERTOPS EVOKE AN EARLY-20TH-CENTURY KITCHEN. THE FACETED CRYSTAL CHANDELIER PROVIDES FANCIFUL CONTRAST TO OTHER ACCESSORIES, WHICH WERE PURPOSELY PARED DOWN FOR A SIMPLER LOOK.

ABOVE THE BEADED-BOARD ISLAND OFFERS A SPOT FOR SNACKS AND FOOD PREPARATION. BECAUSE THIS IS A SUMMER HOME, THE KITCHEN DIDN'T NEED A LOT OF STORAGE, SO WALLS CAN SHOWCASE ARTWORK INSTEAD OF HANGING CABINETS.

PAGE 252 WHITE IN THE MASTER BATH CREATES A TRADITIONAL EFFECT YET MAXIMIZES THE LIGHT.

PAGES 252–253 ARCHED WINDOWS AND FRENCH DOORS OPEN UP THE MASTER BEDROOM. A DRESSING SCREEN BY NICOLA WINGATE-SAUL FEATURES ENGLISH PRINTS, BORDERED IN THE GEORGIAN-IRISH STYLE.

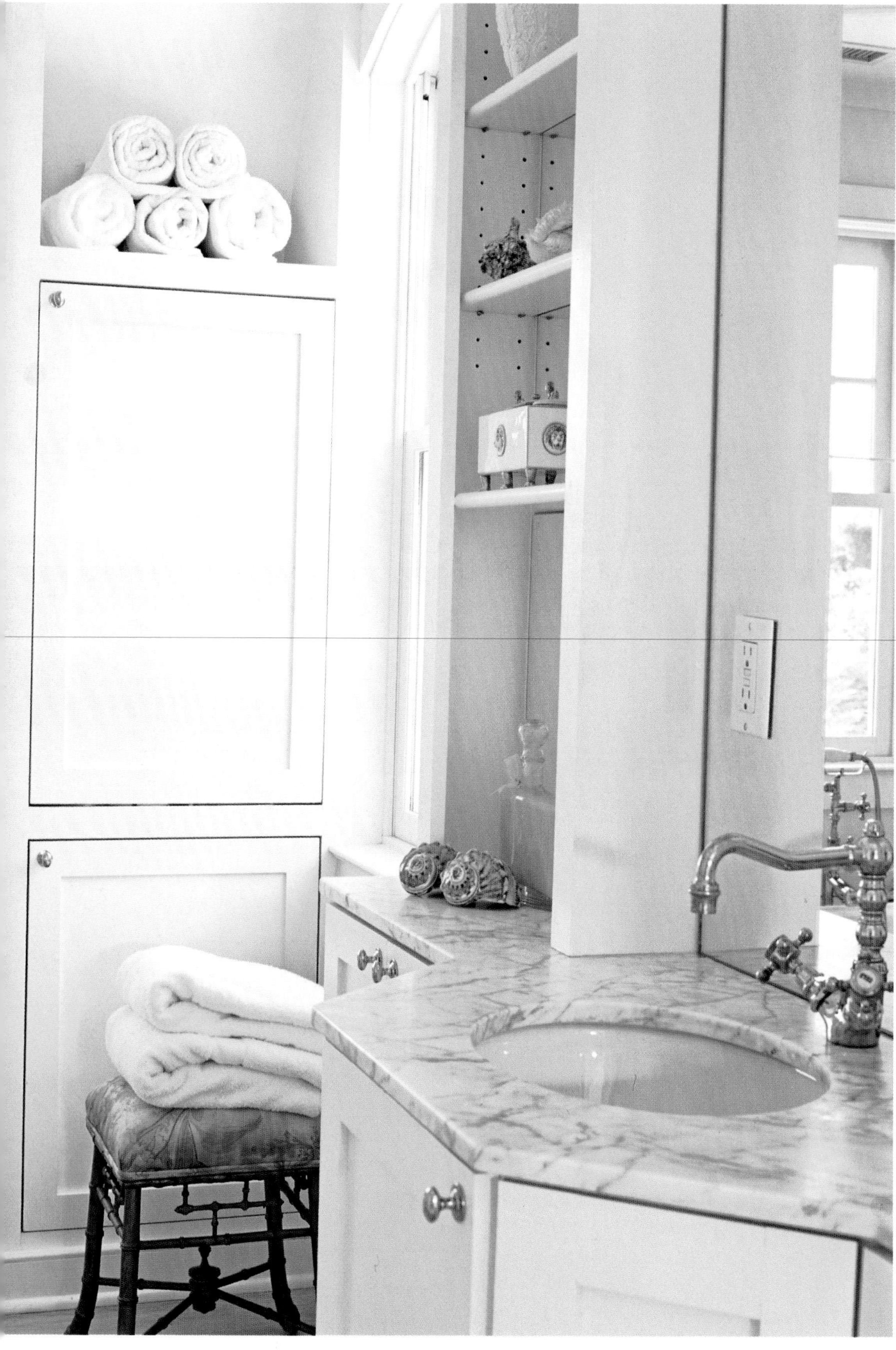

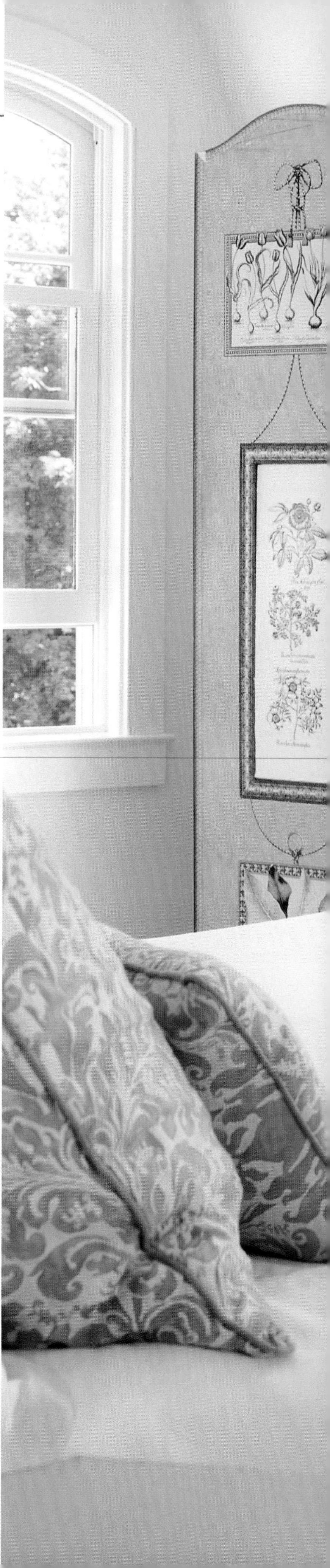

The living room opens to a sunny white kitchen decorated with lemon yellow accents and a sparkling chandelier. Though equipped with the latest appliances, the kitchen has a vintage ambience with beaded-board paneling, countertops of cool marble, and a thick maple butcher block. This room, like the rest of the house, is designed for low maintenance and is almost impervious to sandy footprints.

Upstairs, the master bedroom continues the white-plus-one-color palette; here, the color is a restful blue. The lofty canopy atop an antique English bed swirls toward the ceiling, becoming the room's focal point. The rest is simply furnished, with a decoupage dressing screen serving as art.

"A big part of the project's success is its summertime quality," Disston says. "The family spends a lot of time outdoors. When the house isn't in use, it can be locked up and forgotten about, which is exactly what the owners wanted."

ABOVE A PRISTINE WHITE PERGOLA BRINGS THE ARCHITECTURAL FEATURES OF THE HOUSE OUT INTO THE GARDEN.

RIGHT DOORS ARE OFTEN OPEN IN WARM WEATHER, ALLOWING ACCESS TO THE SCREEN PORCH THAT DOUBLES AS AN OUTDOOR LIVING ROOM. LATTICE OFFERS PRIVACY WITH THE VIEW.

# Repeat Remodeler

Whether it's a trait he was born with or one he acquired, Paul Stepne has a penchant for changing his surroundings—often.

LEFT Small rooms offer the chance to use patterns overwhelming in bigger spaces. The intimate study features a large-scale historically based wallpaper pattern.

OPPOSITE Beautifully polished wood and Chinese porcelain—including one vase made into a lamp—are traditional elements in this home where vivid color prevails.

LEFT SUNNY YELLOW
WALLS AND CRISP WHITE
WOODWORK WARM THE
LIVING ROOM, WHERE
ROSE-COLOR ACCENTS
ECHO REDS IN OTHER
PARTS OF THE HOUSE.
A SMALL CHINESE SCREEN
COVERS THE OPENING OF
THE FIREPLACE WHEN IT'S
NOT IN USE.

For months, the construction debris is everywhere: Piles of lumber and drywall shift from place to place, plumbing fixtures disappear and reappear, and paint cans pop up like bright flowers overnight. The scene seems totally chaotic; then a sustained burst of activity occurs and voilà! Paul Stepne has remodeled another lovely house.

This veteran Minneapolis homeowner thinks that the urge to remodel must be in his blood. "There hasn't been one house that I've walked into without redoing it in my head," he says.

Paul was living in a Craftsman-style bungalow that he had remodeled over the course of three years. One day, he was taking a casual walk around his established neighborhood bordering Lake Harriet. Down the street he spotted a "For Sale" sign in the yard of an outdated two-story Colonial, relatively rare in the Midwest but a reminder of New England transplants who had immigrated to Minnesota. To Paul, the sign was like catnip to a cat. "Well, I had always wanted to do a Colonial with a center hallway," he explains.

Within two weeks, he was happily immersed in his new house—tearing into walls, moving doors a few inches to the side, and adding 200 square feet at the rear. He thrives on making reality conform to his vision, even though while the project was going on, he sometimes had no place to sit down except in his bedroom.

This is the fourth house he has renovated in 10 years. People who know Paul know it won't be the last, though. Just when his neighbors get to see the finished results of his efforts, he'll spot another sign and be up and away again. He loves the process and considers his passion for rescuing outmoded houses and bringing them up to modern standards almost a service. "I feel like I'm giving something back to the community rather than consuming more," Paul says.

Paul's imagination and commitment to quality are key to the uniform success of his projects. In this house, for instance, he determined that he would stay true to its New England

(CONTINUED ON PAGE 264)

RIGHT A STYLIZED CHINOISERIE MURAL, HANDPAINTED BY JUDY STAVROS ON THE WALLS OF THE SUNROOM, CREATES A LIGHTHEARTED ATMOSPHERE FOR FORMAL DINNER PARTIES.

PAGES 262–263 THE STUDY HAS OPULENT WALLPAPER, AN UPDATED 18TH-CENTURY DESIGN IN REDS AND GOLDS. BECAUSE NEIGHBORS LIVE VERY CLOSE, WINDOWS HAVE OPAQUE TEXTURED GLASS INSERTS FOR PRIVACY.

LEFT WITH ITS U-SHAPE CONFIGURATION AND 26 RUNNING FEET OF COUNTERTOP, THE REMODELED KITCHEN IS WELL-SUITED FOR FREQUENT ENTERTAINING.

OPPOSITE VIVID RED IS PAUL'S FAVORITE COLOR BECAUSE IT IS WARMING AND CONVIVIAL. WHITE WOODWORK AND STAINLESS-STEEL APPLIANCES ARE A CLEAN AND AESTHETICALLY PLEASING CONTRAST.

architectural roots. Replacing the rotting clapboards with concrete fiberboard and adding a curving brick walkway were the only significant changes he made to the front elevation. He also left off the black shutters, which were probably a belated addition.

He even decorated his home as though it were occupied by the family of a sea captain who had traveled the world and had brought back treasures from the Orient. Beginning by converting a former dining room to a study, he transformed each room with broad sweeps of strong color—imperial yellow and Mandarin red. In this setting, his gleaming wood furniture, traditional upholstered pieces, and Asian porcelains attract the attention they deserve.

To further heighten the Colonial-era ambience, Paul had a friend, artist Judy Stavros, paint the walls of the sunroom with a simplified chinoiserie design. Dramatic pagoda roofs and wispy trees now surround the guests when Paul hosts his frequent dinner parties.

The rest of his home adheres to the red and yellow scheme—even the kitchen, where crimson walls find their complements in sleek steel, fresh white cabinets, and a slate-look floor. Only upstairs in the master bedroom addition did Paul tone it down a bit with slightly subdued colors. This is so he can rest peacefully—undoubtedly dreaming of projects to come.

ABOVE WHEN HE FIRST SAW THIS SUBSTANTIAL REPRODUCTION SINK, PAUL FELL IN LOVE. HE DECIDED TO ABANDON HIS BATH BUDGET AND TAKE THE PLUNGE.

RIGHT THE MASTER BEDROOM HAS A MASCULINE MIX OF POLISHED MAHOGANY, NATURAL TEXTURES, AND EARTHY TONES.

# Family Endeavor

## An interior designer helps his parents transform a seasonal lake house into a comfortable year-round home.

LEFT A CLOVERLEAF-SHAPE OTTOMAN SERVES AS FOOTSTOOL, SEATING, AND COFFEE TABLE IN THE FAMILY ROOM.

OPPOSITE BLUE, WHITE, AND YELLOW—THAT CLASSIC PALETTE—WAS CHOSEN FOR THE DINING ROOM BY CONSENSUS. THE SLIPCOVERED CHAIRS REVERT TO CARAMEL-COLOR LEATHER FOR THE WINTER MONTHS.

LEFT FLORAL FABRICS
AND PASTEL COLORS
GIVE THE LAKE HOUSE
AN ENGLISH-COTTAGE
LOOK. FLOWER PAINTINGS
IN GILDED FRAMES
UNDERSCORE THE
FLORAL THEME. TERRA-
COTTA DEER AND AN
ANTLER CHANDELIER
RECALL THE ORIGINAL
FUNCTION OF THE HOUSE
AS A HUNTING LODGE.

Spending summers at the lake was a tradition for the Aman family. They enjoyed its serenity, its private setting, and the way it had reverted to single-family cottages after a period of hosting rambling lakeside hotels. So when Marcia and James Aman decided to live at the New Jersey lake year-round, they knew they could easily relax into the lifestyle they love.

Their unwinterized cottage wouldn't do, though, so they and their grown son, Jim Aman, searched for a larger, more permanent place. They finally found it—a former hunting lodge called Deer Cottage, built in the 1920s with tongue-and-groove paneling, vaulted ceilings, and—best of all—its own boathouse, a luxury no longer allowed for new construction.

The structure had been neglected over the years, as one renter after another had come and gone. Luckily, the Amans could again call on Jim, a New York-based interior designer who with his partner, Ann Carson, took on the project of fixing it up and making it suit his family.

"As soon as I walked in, I fell in love with the two stone fireplaces and the vaulted ceilings, and I loved having the

RIGHT PAINTED
V-GROOVE PANELING
LIGHTENS UP THE
FORMERLY DARK DINING
ROOM, WHERE A MIX
OF PLAIDS AND PRINTS
ECHOES THE COBALT
BLUE AND WHITE OF
MARCIA'S PRIZED
PORCELAIN. TROMPE
L'OEIL PAINTINGS OVER
THE WINDOW AND ON THE
MANTEL HUMOROUSLY
MIMIC A PAIR OF DELFT
URNS AND SEVERAL
VINTAGE SILHOUETTES.

water views," Marcia says. "The work the house needed was really mostly cosmetic. We made no architectural changes."

Being their son's clients was a different role for the two—who had their own opinions regarding the decorating style for their new home. These didn't always mesh with Jim's professional choices, so the stage was set for some family give-and-take.

"There were definitely some compromises," explains Marcia. "I love flowers everywhere, and that wasn't necessarily Jim's taste. I fought him on a lot of things, but

LEFT EASY-TO-REMOVE
FLORAL SLIPCOVERS,
MARCIA'S PREFERENCE,
LET HER CHANGE THE
FAMILY ROOM DECOR
WITH THE SEASONS. THE
TREFOIL OTTOMAN—
LARGE, BUT QUITE
PRACTICAL—SERVES AS
A COFFEE TABLE AND
A GIANT FOOTSTOOL.
MINIATURES OF ANTIQUE
CHAIRS GRACE THE
MANTEL BENEATH A
GILDED-BAMBOO MIRROR.

then I realized he was probably right." The older Amans were unaccustomed to letting their son make so many decisions. The situation required Jim to persuade them gently and explain the rationale behind certain things.

On one point, Marcia wouldn't compromise. She insisted on bringing her beloved antiques and collections because they had been such a part of her life. The English secretary, antique bamboo chairs, and an extensive collection of blue-and-white porcelain had to be worked into the plan.

Ann says that this helped set the course of the project; knowing that the goal was to make the place look more like a permanent home than a lake house, she and Jim could use more formal fabrics and let the details shine.

Mother and son finally agreed that pretty fabrics—including florals—would be used in every room, especially in the master bedroom and family room. The proviso, though, was that other rooms would wear their flowers only in the spring and summer, and that slipcovers were the answer.

About the bedroom, Jim laughs and says, "My mother adores that room; my father tolerates it," raising suspicions

LEFT FLORAL MOTIFS
AND RICKRACK-TRIMMED
LINENS RECALL A CASUAL,
GARDEN-STYLE COTTAGE
IN THE MASTER BEDROOM.
HAND-PAINTED FLOWERS
BLOOM ON THE SPACIOUS
BUILT-IN STORAGE UNIT.

OPPOSITE WHITE
BEADED BOARD
AND MARBLE JOIN
REPRODUCTION FIXTURES
IN THE "VICTORIAN" BATH.
GOLD-FRAMED CHERUBS
AND A FANCIFUL CHAIR
ADD A BIT OF WARMTH.

that male family members may have conspired. But perhaps not. "This is our only home," Marcia says, "and I like changing it with the seasons."

The dining room needn't rely on fabric for its flowers; it has a steady supply because Marcia is an avid gardener. Chairs and a carved antique English table anchor the room. Slipcovers here transform the chairs from mellow golden leather to cool plaids that mirror the blue porcelain.

A custom-made antler chandelier, Austrian terra-cotta replicas of deer, and paintings based on the history of the lake set an outdoorsy tone in the living room. The ambience changes from rustic fireside living to living in a bower, though, as soon as daffodils rear their heads.

Both Marcia and James enjoy the yearly transformation that takes place when winter gives up and spring rushes in to refresh their spirits. Their home is also refreshed, and soon it's filled with friends and family seeking fun on the water. "Our lives are much more peaceful now that we live here year-round," Marcia says. James and Jim agree.

# Summer Idyll

## A California couple seeks to recapture the simple pleasures of childhood summers in Minnesota.

LEFT HYDRANGEAS COME FROM THE GARDEN BLOOMING RIGHT OUTSIDE THE DOORS OF THE BREAKFAST ROOM.

OPPOSITE AN ENDEARING FOUNTAIN STANDS PERMANENT WATCH OVER A LILY POND POPULATED BY GOLDFISH.

OPPOSITE CHAIRS IN A CHIPPED-PAINT FINISH ADD INFORMAL CHIC TO THE LIVING ROOM. APPLE GREEN WALLS CREATE A YOUNG-AT-HEART AIR.

RIGHT ALTHOUGH INTERPRETED IN WOOD INSTEAD OF BRICK, THE ARCHITECTURAL ELEMENTS—A SYMMETRICAL FACADE, SHUTTERED WINDOWS, A PORTICOED DOOR WITH AN ORANGE-SLICE WINDOW AND SIDELIGHTS—REVEAL THE STRUCTURE'S TRADITIONAL ROOTS.

California seems like home now to Jamie and Scott Honour, because they have lived there more than 10 years. Enjoying its mild climate, they built busy lives in the Los Angeles area. Every once in a while, though, they have felt the urge to return to Minneapolis, where they both grew up, to refresh their spirits and catch up with relatives still in the Midwest.

Then came parenthood. Two sons arrived in as many years—Everett, 3, and Owen, 2. It became increasingly hard to pack up the boys for trips back to Minnesota, and the family had to take along their three puppies too. "It was getting a little cramped [bunking down] in my mother-in-law's basement," Scott says with a laugh.

The couple feels strongly about family ties, though. "We wanted our kids to have all the fond memories that we had, spending time with their grandparents," says Jamie, who is a full-time mom. After a lot of discussion, they decided to purchase a summer home near Minneapolis so the boys could have long, uninterrupted stretches of time with their extended family. Scott works as an investment banker and has enough flexibility to commute between cities as necessary.

The Honours were ecstatic when their real estate broker showed them an online listing for a homey 1920s yellow clapboard house in the Minneapolis suburb of Edina; it was only blocks from where Jamie grew up. It had all the charm of the homes they remembered, yet

RIGHT DESPITE ITS
PRETTY APPEARANCE,
THE BREAKFAST ROOM IS
ALMOST TODDLER-PROOF.
LAMINATED FABRIC
CUSHIONS WIPE CLEAN
EASILY, AND THE TILE
FLOOR IS IMPERVIOUS TO
SPILLED MILK.

FAR RIGHT STAINLESS-
STEEL COUNTERTOPS AND
A PROFESSIONAL RANGE
ARE SOPHISTICATED
NOTES IN THE COTTAGE-
STYLE KITCHEN. WALLS
OF V-GROOVE PANELING
ADD AN OFFHAND CHARM,
REMINISCENT OF A
REMODELED PORCH.

it also had a recent two-story addition with an up-to-date
kitchen and family room on the ground floor and a spacious
master suite on the second floor. Even the summer-fresh
color scheme of yellow and green was pleasing to them. So
they visited the home. "From the moment I walked in the
front door, I knew it was for us," Jamie says. "It felt like an
old friend."

Period details in the addition are in keeping with the age
of the original house. Black and white tile in the kitchen,
antique light fixtures, and tongue-and-groove ceilings add
character. French doors along the back overlook a charming
garden with hydrangeas, rhododendrons, a pergola, and a

OPPOSITE A TONGUE-AND-GROOVE VAULTED CEILING INTRODUCES AN AIRY, COTTAGE QUALITY TO THE MASTER BEDROOM. FLORAL-EMBROIDERED LINENS AND LUSCIOUS SHERBET COLORS HEIGHTEN THE SUN-KISSED EFFECT.

RIGHT A SYMMETRICAL ARRANGEMENT OF FRAMED FERN PRINTS BRINGS THE OUTDOORS INTO THE UPSTAIRS HALL.

lily-filled pond—home to goldfish that fascinate the boys. "We live a lot of our lives outside," Scott says, "and the French doors provide a very easy flow in and out for entertaining."

Local interior designer Debra Martinson, who had worked with the previous occupants, helped Jamie with the decorating. Martinson explains, "This home is centered around sunshine, light colors, and flowers." The two decided to keep yellow and green as the basic colors; then they added a little more masculinity in deference to the three "men" of the house. A change of paint in several rooms and a few darker furnishings was all it took for the home to suit everyone.

The children don't understand all that. All they know is that when it's time to leave for Minnesota, they're so excited they can hardly wait. "Our kids are happy. We're happy," Jamie says. "That house just does something special to us when we're there."